Executive Coaching

A Psychodynamic Approach

C000301081

Coaching in Practice series

The aim of this series is to help coaching professionals gain a broader understanding of the challenges and issues they face in coaching, enabling them to make the leap from being a 'good-enough' coach to an outstanding one. This series is an essential aid for both the novice coach eager to learn how to grow a coaching practice, and the more experienced coach looking for new knowledge and strategies. Combining theory with practice, the series provides a comprehensive guide to becoming successful in this rapidly expanding profession.

Published and forthcoming titles:

Bluckert: *Psychological Dimensions of Coaching*
Brown & Brown: *Coaching the Mind and Brain*
Driver: *Coaching Positively*
Hawkins: *Coaching Strategy in Organizations*
Hay: *Reflective Practice and Supervision for Coaches*
Hayes: *NLP Coaching*
Rogers: *Developing a Coaching Business*
Vaughan Smith: *Therapist into Coach*

Executive Coaching

A Psychodynamic Approach

Catherine Sandler

 Open University Press

Open University Press
McGraw-Hill Education
McGraw-Hill House
Shoppenhangers Road
Maidenhead
Berkshire
England
SL6 2QL

email: enquiries@openup.co.uk
world wide web: www.openup.co.uk

and Two Penn Plaza, New York, NY 10121-2289, USA

First published 2011

Copyright © Catherine Sandler 2011

All rights reserved. Except for the quotation of short passages for the purpose of criticism and review, no part of this publication may be reproduced, stored in a retrieval system, or transmitted, in any form or by any means, electronic, mechanical, photocopying, recording or otherwise, without the prior written permission of the publisher or a licence from the Copyright Licensing Agency Limited. Details of such licences (for reprographic reproduction) may be obtained from the Copyright Licensing Agency Ltd of Saffron House, 6–10 Kirby Street, London EC1N 8TS.

A catalogue record of this book is available from the British Library

ISBN: 978-0-33-523793-7 (pb) 978-0-33-523792-0 (hb)
eISBN: 978-0-33-524040-1

Library of Congress Cataloging-in-Publication Data
CIP data applied for

Typeset by RefineCatch Limited, Bungay, Suffolk
Printed in the UK by Ashford Colour Press., Gosport, Hampshire.

Fictitious names of companies, products, people, characters and/or data that may be used herein (in case studies or in examples) are not intended to represent any real individual, company, product or event.

The McGraw·Hill Companies

Contents

This book is dedicated to
Martin, Simon, Rachel, Danny and Zoë

Series Editor's Foreword

Executive coaching has been around now for many decades and has become a popular second career for many senior people who themselves have been coached. When you see coaching done well it looks easy and seamless but this is the art that conceals art. Most beginner coaches soon find that they face a dilemma: the client states that they want to change and they mean it most sincerely, and yet somehow the really profound changes do not occur – things do get a little better, but the heavy routines of overwork continue, the inability to delegate remains more or less as it was, the oppressive task-driven boss is still at risk of being seen as a bully, and so on. What is going on here?

Simplistic approaches to coaching will not provide the answers. For instance, learning a few 'techniques', as so often offered by those organizations that promise you can become a full-fledged coach in a weekend, is never enough. And for many years much of the training and writing about coaching has been based essentially on a behavioural approach: discuss the problem, agree what the goal is, talk about the behaviour that will mean the goal is being achieved, do the behaviour and hey presto, the problem is solved! Alas, this is not often how it is in reality.

Catherine Sandler's book will help you as a coach to understand why human beings resist the very changes they say they want to make. Drawing on the rich tradition of psychoanalysis, she describes how psychodynamic insights, translated into practical strategies, can be the key to working with clients to move them on in a transformational rather than a transactional way. The true reason that we find change so difficult is that we have developed and perfected any number of defensive tactics to keep us exactly as we are. These are defences against anxiety and we all have them, even those well-functioning, stable and highly successful people in senior roles in organizations who appear in our lives as clients.

Catherine's book is a practical, readable guide, written by one of the UK's most experienced and successful executive coaches. In it she explains, with the help of many case studies drawn from her practice, how to apply psychodynamic ideas. Many coaches are unnecessarily fearful of therapeutic ideas and their application to coaching. This book will convince you that in calling on these powerful approaches and ideas, while you are not doing therapy you will nonetheless be far better equipped to work with clients at a new level of complexity and effectiveness. Her helpful models and easily followed explanations are the best introduction I know to ideas that could transform your practice as a coach.

The book is also a reminder that in executive coaching there are essentially two lines of accountability: the client him or herself and the organization for which he or she works. Managing that duality is a subtle task in itself – you always have to know how to work with the client as well as with the system in which he or she operates. Again, this book will be a reliable guide to steering yourself through the many possible traps that could otherwise engulf you.

The world of coaching has needed this book for some years and I am delighted to have been part of its gestation.

Jenny Rogers
Series Editor

Acknowledgements

This is a welcome opportunity to thank those people whose help and support have contributed to this book becoming a reality. They number many and I can mention only a few by name.

Kate Lanz, Brenda Ross, Colette Gannon, Jani Rubery and Rachel Goodwin, my coaching colleagues at Sandler Lanz, have contributed to my thinking over many years through the regular exchange of ideas and practice. Their professionalism, loyalty and commitment to doing the best possible work for each client has made working as a team a source of pride and pleasure. My special thanks go to Kate for her outstanding capacity for collaboration and unfailing friendship.

Grateful thanks are also due to Anne Rabbit, the Sandler Lanz office manager, who runs our practice with such care and skill, ably supported by Bianca Barbu and Zoshia Nowicki. They make delegation easy and without them I would not have had the peace of mind to concentrate on this book.

Thanks, too, to my two understanding editors. Jenny Rogers has provided excellent stylistic advice and both she and Monika Lee have been encouraging and patient with me throughout the writing process. My supervisor, Tricia Barnes, has provided me with the highest calibre of support, sustaining my confidence and keeping me on the right path.

My mother, Anne-Marie Sandler, and my late father, Joseph Sandler, have each made unique contributions to this book. They provided ambitious role models and brought me up to look beyond the surface. My mother has given me generous help with the theoretical aspects of the psychodynamic model (any mistakes are mine alone) and my father, whose own writing is so clear and incisive, always wanted me to produce a book. Although he is not here to see it, I know he would be happy and proud.

My own family deserve special mention. Without the active encouragement of my husband, Martin Dedman, this book would not have been started, let alone finished. For his insistence that I get going, his belief in my ability, his helpful comments on my drafts and for taking such superb care of our daily domestic and culinary needs, he has my warmest thanks and love. My older daughter, Rachel, who helped edit the text with a deftness and maturity beyond her years, has been a special source of support. Simon, Danny and Zoë have shown great tolerance for the absences, both physical and psychological, which writing a book seems inevitably to entail. Fortunately for us all, Zoë's beloved puppy, Roo, provided excellent compensation.

ACKNOWLEDGEMENTS

Finally, I would like to thank the coaching clients and supervisees with whom I have had the privilege to work over the past two decades. Through them, I have developed the thinking and skills described in this book and have learnt a great deal about myself. I have been touched and inspired by their honesty, courage and capacity for attachment and change. I hold them in mind with gratitude and affection.

Preface

This book has had a long gestation period. I have worked in the field of leadership development for over twenty years and have wanted to write about what I do for quite some time. Yet the demands of building a business, working with clients and bringing up a family have meant that this enterprise has had to wait its turn. My fiftieth birthday in 2008 provided a spur. My children were growing up, my practice was in good shape and I felt that I was ready to describe my work with clarity and confidence.

Within a few weeks of having my book proposal accepted, the UK went into recession. As many of the organizations I work with grappled with the shock of tumbling profits, budget cuts and sweeping redundancies – with some companies fighting for survival – my full attention turned to my clients and my business. While this delayed the start of this book, it proved a surprisingly creative period. Kate Lanz and I found ourselves busy engaging with senior teams and individuals on the theme of *leading in turbulent times*. The thinking that this prompted resulted in the development of two models, one of which focused on the psychological role of the leader in maintaining morale during a downturn (Sandler, 2009b). The second model, the Emotional Profiles Triangle, deals with how leaders handle pressure and is presented here.

Early in 2010, with the editors beginning to wonder if this book would ever materialize, I started writing. The process of examining just what I do when I coach has been an exacting one. It has served to enhance my own awareness and helped me to improve my practice. I have also welcomed the chance to offer other coaches what may be a fresh perspective and the opportunity to try something new. I have always loved teaching and supervision, and writing has offered this pleasure in a different form.

Catherine Sandler

Introduction

This book is designed for executive coaches and allied professionals who would like to learn more about psychodynamic psychology and how it can be applied to executive coaching. If your role involves enabling others to develop – whether as consultant, therapist, counsellor, mentor, educator, HR professional, manager or leader – there are concepts, strategies and techniques here that could help you extend and enhance your practice (I use the term HR to refer to professionals in the areas of human resources, learning and development, and talent management).

Executive coaches work in a wide variety of different ways, so the approach that I describe in this book is my own. In explaining the influence of psychodynamic theory on my coaching, I aim to build a bridge between ideas and action. The emphasis is on practical application; examples and case studies are provided throughout. Although I work mainly with senior leaders, this material is relevant to any coaching client who has responsibility for leading, managing or influencing others. I hope that you will find within it some aspects that you can incorporate into your own work.

The psychodynamic approach: explaining the value, dispelling the myths

The psychodynamic perspective is not the only one I bring to my practice. I also draw on ideas from the fields of organizational behaviour, leadership and management theory, neuroscience, personality type, cognitive behavioural therapy, group dynamics and systems thinking, among others. Yet the psychodynamic model makes a unique contribution. It enables me to help clients achieve their specific coaching goals while undergoing the psychological and emotional changes needed to underpin their long-term success. As a result, they achieve in-depth and sustainable improvements in performance that will last throughout their careers and benefit both their current and future organizations. The purpose of this book is to bring this process alive.

In doing so, I aim to dispel some powerful myths about the psychodynamic model that may have put you off in the past. First, I intend to show how psychodynamic ideas can be applied to the issues that the client faces in their work *without in-depth exploration of their personal history*. Many people assume that any approach that draws on psychoanalytic theory inevitably involves considerable reference to the individual's childhood, parental relationships and upbringing. In my practice, this is not the case. As the book will demonstrate, I explore the client's *current performance at work* and apply psychodynamic concepts to understanding their characteristic emotional and behavioural patterns and how these impact on their leadership and management abilities. I also use psychodynamic insights to frame my side of the coaching conversation as effectively as possible.

A second myth is that only those trained in psychoanalysis, psycho-therapy or counselling can make appropriate use of psychodynamic ideas. Although it is true that the psychodynamic model is relatively little known or used outside these specialized fields, I believe that it has an immense amount to offer non-clinicians in fields such as coaching when it is applied with thoughtfulness and care. (There are professional centres in the UK and abroad where the psychodynamic perspective is applied to work with organizations, including the Tavistock Consultancy Service, but these are few and far between.) There are some provisos, though. If you are interested in using these ideas, as well as being open-minded and reflective, it is important to be as self-aware as possible. To this end, I would strongly suggest seeking experiential learning opportunities, whether through group relations events, therapy or counselling or other forms of development. Good-quality coaching supervision is also vital.

Third, the book addresses the myth that a psychodynamic approach will necessarily be more concerned with the client's personal needs than the needs of their organization, that it may in effect be a disguised form of psychotherapy. Psychodynamically influenced executive coaching has a different purpose and context from those of therapy and counselling. The aim of executive coaching is to help clients *improve their performance at work* for the benefit of their organization as well as themselves. To this end, my focus is on enabling them to become as effective and successful as possible *in the context of their professional role and business goals*. Indeed, the importance of the executive coach's dual accountability – to the individual and to their organization – is emphasized and explored in this book. Although some clients may well experience benefits elsewhere in their lives as a result of coaching, this is regarded as a bonus.

Therapy and counselling, on the other hand, address emotional or psy-chological problems, often stemming from childhood, which interfere with the individual's ability to enjoy life, sustain successful relationships or cope with everyday challenges and pressures. They help with conditions such as anxiety or depression or destabilizing life events such as bereavement. A good coach will understand this and have the capacity to recognize when a client should be referred on to a therapist or other professional should they need this kind of support (Buckley and Buckley, 2006) (this topic is also touched upon in Chapter 11, p. 159).

Key influences on my coaching

To provide some context for the presence of the psychodynamic approach at the heart of my practice, I shall briefly share some of the highlights of my professional journey. Like most coaches, the way I work has been shaped by several powerful influences.

Having started my graduate life in academia, I quickly discovered through starting to teach evening classes that I was more interested in helping adults learn than in doing research. I took a full-time job with the Workers' Educational Association where I designed and ran a programme called 'Second Chance to Learn' for adults who had left school with no qualifications and who were unemployed. This consisted of group work combined with one-to-one support – a prototype form of coaching. The process of containing these students' anxiety, engaging them in learning, building their confidence and enabling them to succeed, often for the first time in their lives, was deeply rewarding. Not a single student dropped out of the pilot course and all went on to further education, to find jobs or to set up their own businesses. When the programme was over I knew that I wanted to work with adults in a developmental role of some kind.

In the period that followed, having taken a year out to complete my thesis, I attended an enriching variety of programmes in the fields of interpersonal training and applied psychology. In 1987, I participated in the Leicester Conference, an entirely experiential two-week residential learning event run by the Tavistock Clinic, a centre of psychodynamic psychology with a world-class reputation, in conjunction with the Tavistock Institute. Extraordinarily intense, it was a powerful way to learn about the visible and hidden dynamics of groups, large and small, and about myself. Intrigued by the application of these ideas to organizational life, I went on to spend two years in Paris working for a Tavistock-influenced French management consultancy whose main client was the nationalized utilities giant EDF-GDF (Électricité de France – Gaz de France).

These experiences were not my first exposure to the psycho-dynamic approach, however. This had begun much earlier. My parents were both psychoanalysts so I grew up surrounded by the assumption that our early experiences are important and that emotions such as anxiety, anger and guilt play a meaningful part in driving our behaviour. Although the practice of clinical psychoanalysis has never appealed – and I could not honestly recommend having two psychoanalysts as parents – my background contributed significantly to my interest in human behaviour. Moreover, when I had some psychotherapy myself in my twenties, I found it immensely helpful both in relation to specific issues and as a means of understanding myself.

In 1989, having returned to London to marry and start a family, I developed a freelance career in the field of leadership development. In 1993, Brenda Ross introduced me to her colleagues at the London Business School and for the next seven years I worked there regularly, coaching groups of executives from companies as diverse as Morgan Stanley, Roche Pharmaceuticals and British Aerospace. I also taught and coached on open courses from the MBA to the Senior Executive Programme. I learned to use a wide range of psychometric and behavioural instruments and was exposed to the latest thinking and practice in the field of management and leadership development. This work immersed me in the business challenges and organizational issues facing those in the private sector and provided an invaluable apprenticeship.

In 2000, I helped to introduce a module focusing on individual leadership development for executives studying at the INSEAD Global Leadership Centre. This quickly became a central feature of all its open and company-specific programmes. The IGLC takes a psychodynamic approach to executive education and I remained involved in this fascinating international work until a few years ago when the demands of my UK practice left little time for trips to Paris. During this time I also taught and supervised on the Tavistock Clinic's MA course in organizational development and did some extremely interesting work in association with the Tavistock Consultancy Service.

Alongside teaching, consulting and coaching in these different organizational settings, I continued to develop my interest in individual psychology. In the early 1990s, I trained and qualified as a counsellor at Regent's College in London and ran a small psychodynamically oriented practice for three years alongside my other work. This experience was helpful in crystallizing my preference for coaching and consulting. While counselling was challenging and worthwhile, I realized just how much I enjoyed working with highly functional individuals in leadership roles and helping them to navigate the complexities of organizational and business life.

Out of this diversity of experience emerged the decision to focus on one-to-one coaching. I felt that I could bring a powerful combination of business understanding and psychological expertise to my clients and their organizations and in 1998 I founded Sandler Consulting. I began to work with executives from the retail, banking, transport and pharmaceutical sectors and from professional partnerships in the fields of accountancy and law. As well as coaching, I provided an increasing amount of coaching supervision as the field began to expand. In 2004, when coaching at INSEAD, I met Kate Lanz and within less than a fortnight she was doing an outstanding job of coaching a particularly challenging client in my practice. From then on we worked closely together. In 2007, we went into partnership as Sandler Lanz and have continued to specialize in executive coaching with business leaders and senior teams.

The structure of the book

Chapter 1 provides the context for the rest of this book by introducing executive coaching and the main features of my coaching practice. Chapters 2 and 3 set out the key tenets of psychodynamic theory and spell out the implications for my work. Chapters 4 and 5 address the heart of the coaching process: how to build a relationship with the client, enable them to feel safe enough to learn, help them develop insight and promote productive change. Chapter 6 examines the implications of the coach's dual accountability to both individual and organization and how the early interactions with the organization at the start of the process can be the source of useful data.

Chapter 7 introduces the Emotional Profiles Triangle (EPT), which provides a simple but powerful framework for understanding three styles of leadership and how each kind of leader behaves under pressure. I explain how the EPT can be used as an effective and versatile coaching tool. Chapters 8, 9 and 10 consist of client case studies, each of which illustrates one of the EPT profiles. Chapter 11 examines an important but often overlooked aspect of coaching – the ending – and also touches on the related issues of attachment and dependency.

Client material

There is one more point that I would like to draw the reader's attention to at the outset. It concerns the client material that appears throughout this book, illustrating the ideas and techniques that I use in coaching. Three chapters consist entirely of client case studies. If I have done my job well, these stories will be realistic and convincing. I must emphasize, however, that every client described is entirely fictional. In creating each character, I have drawn on my work over many years with scores of individuals whose issues have been similar to those in the examples.

In the course of writing, some of these fictional clients – Sebastian, Daniel and Nicola in particular – have taken on a life of their own and I have grown fond of them. I would like to think that this reflects the realistic nature of the thoughts, feelings, strengths, weaknesses, challenges and triumphs with which they have been endowed. I hope you will enjoy meeting them.

1 What is executive coaching?

Sebastian was a talented lawyer with excellent technical and client skills whose career risked being derailed by his aggressive behaviour in the office; **Daniel** was a likeable senior manager in the pharmaceutical industry who enjoyed team-building but struggled to deal with poor performers and difficult colleagues; and **Nicola** was a Managing Director in the financial services sector who preferred strategic planning to people management and had received feedback that her team found her too remote. All three are typical of the clients with whom I work. They came into executive coaching to become more effective leaders by addressing the issues that were limiting their success. All were helped, along with their organizations, by the application of a psychodynamic perspective. Their coaching stories are told in the last three chapters of this book.

As these stories will reveal, coaching can be a deceptively challenging process for all concerned. Human beings find change difficult. We want change but we also fear and resist it. Clients may enter coaching enthusiastically, be genuinely keen to find new ways of functioning, yet prove stubbornly resistant to relinquishing their old ways. Some prove incapable of gaining real insight into themselves or others. Some gain insight and embrace fresh skills but seem unable to apply them to real situations at work. Others commit themselves to new behavioural strategies but fail repeatedly to carry them through.

This is one of the reasons why I find the psychodynamic approach so powerful. It provides a fascinating conceptual lens through which to understand the human mind. It explains the complex and deep-rooted nature of the emotional and behavioural patterns that we develop over our lifetimes – and why we persist with these patterns, even when they do not serve us well. Psychodynamic thinking also highlights the need to bring a subtle and thoughtful approach to every aspect of my coaching work. It has enhanced my ability to establish close and fruitful relationships with clients, to help them leverage their strengths and to address those underlying factors that prevent them from achieving their full potential.

My coaching practice

My purpose when coaching is to provide a powerful developmental experience for the individual that will generate clear benefits for their organization. I aim to help clients become more effective, confident and fulfilled in their roles and more successful in meeting their objectives. Before explaining the psychodynamic model and illustrating how it helps me to achieve this, I shall briefly share some key features of my practice. This is designed to provide an introduction for those of you who are new to this area and to clarify how executive coaching differs from other forms of coaching. It will also provide a context for the material that follows. Here are some practical facts about the way I work:

- It is almost always the client's organization that commissions and funds the coaching.
- I generally work with clients for between six and twelve months.
- Coaching sessions take place at my offices, away from the pressures and distractions of the client's everyday environment.
- Coaching sessions take place at approximately three to four week intervals.
- A coaching session typically lasts for two hours.
- I stay in regular contact with my clients between sessions.

Who are my clients and how and why do they come into coaching?

The individuals I work with come into coaching for a range of reasons and through different routes. Senior leaders may be facing a particularly challenging period or strategic organizational task and feel that coaching will help them perform at their best. Executives at all levels may have undergone a 360-degree feedback process or taken part in a leadership programme and identified areas of their performance that they feel are hindering the delivery of their business goals.[1] Some are keen to use coaching to clarify career goals and accelerate their progress within their organization. Others struggle with anxiety, overload and stress of various kinds at work and look to coaching to help them learn to cope more effectively. CEOs and those near the top of their organizations who may have few peers in whom to confide may be seeking an external, confidential 'thought partner'. The most senior clients tend to commission coaching for themselves, although this is often done with the help and involvement of senior Human Resources (HR) colleagues. Less senior executives may also initiate coaching themselves. They usually come from companies that use coaching regularly and they will initiate the process by requesting it via their line-manager or HR partner.

Anna

A good example of a self-starting client was **Anna**. Newly-appointed Managing Director of a wholly-owned subsidiary of an international insurance company, she faced the challenge of turning round the performance of a business which was failing to meet its targets in an increasingly competitive marketplace. She felt isolated and a little overwhelmed and decided that an executive coach with whom she could share her concerns would help her stay reflective and resourced despite the pressure of a huge workload. She was also keen to hone her influencing skills and leadership impact, both areas in which she felt she performed quite well but wanted to become excellent. Acting on an acquaintance's recommendation, she called me herself and we arranged an initial consultation which led to an agreement to work together.

Many clients, however, do not initiate coaching. Instead, it is offered or proposed to them by their boss or the HR professionals within their organization. This happens for different reasons. Often the individual is being prepared for – or has already moved into – a more senior role. They may be in line for succession to a key post or about to take charge of a particularly critical area or project. Coaching is designed to help them navigate these transitions as rapidly and effectively as possible and to accelerate their performance in the new context. For example, coaching is often deployed when an executive is taking up their first role on the Board of their company, to support them in making the crucial shift from operational to strategic leadership. Other clients enter coaching to improve their skills and effectiveness in areas such as people management, team-building, influencing, communication, handling conflict, delegation and work/life balance. Many individuals also want to develop greater confidence, gravitas and leadership impact. Sometimes clients are established players who are regarded as bringing great value to the organization but who are struggling with a particular aspect of their performance, such as business development. Sometimes coaching is simply a vote of confidence, showing that the organization sees them as high-potential and is keen to invest in their development.

Although this category of client has not proactively requested coaching, they are usually open to the idea and many are pleased to have been offered the opportunity. In the early days of executive coaching, some clients felt that there was a stigma attached to coaching, seeing it primarily as a remedial process, but over the past few years this attitude has changed significantly.

Raj

Raj was a client for whom coaching was proposed by his organization. A senior manager within a large retail bank, he was seen as having great potential but was considered stronger on the technical side than as a people leader. He had been invited to step into his boss's role while she was on maternity leave.

It was felt that this would give him a valuable opportunity to develop his management and strategic skills and build his confidence. Coaching was seen as an essential element in helping him step up to this challenge and prepare him for eventual promotion. Raj welcomed the chance to have coaching. Although the idea made him feel a little apprehensive, he enjoyed meeting his coach and engaged quickly in the process.

Finally, there is a third category of client comprising those who are *sent* for coaching by their organization in order to address one or more particular issues. Their response to the idea of coaching ranges from compliance to resistance. In some cases, this means that coaching has little chance of success. In others, a difficult or unpromising start can lead to surprisingly good results. In these situations, I work closely with the organization to assess whether coaching is likely to be the best intervention for all concerned. If appropriate, I suggest an alternative strategy.

Elizabeth

In the case of **Elizabeth**, a national director responsible for fund-raising within a large charity, coaching was effectively imposed. A hard-working, task-focused individual who did not handle stress well, a personal problem outside work had contributed to her management style becoming increasingly abrasive. Morale in her team was at rock-bottom and performance was suffering. A series of feedback conversations between the head of the charity and Elizabeth culminated in the threat of formal disciplinary proceedings unless her behaviour changed. Coaching was put forward as a necessary step in order to help her manage her moods and behaviour and improve her management style. Elizabeth reluctantly agreed. Despite this difficult start, coaching played a vital part in enabling her to recalibrate her moods and behaviour and improve her team's results.

The challenges of working one-to-one

In helping all these clients to address their coaching goals, the executive coach faces a unique challenge. We work on a one-to-one basis with the individual yet our main focus is on their performance within a complex organizational system.[2] Every organization has its own purpose, structure, culture and history but our experience of these is primarily at one remove. To assess the impact of these factors on the client's thoughts, emotions and behaviour, we must gather as much information about their organization as possible. As well as speaking with the client's boss and liaising with members of the HR function, I visit their offices, do thorough desk research and follow the fortunes of the organization through the media. I also use my own experience of interacting with each organization as an external partner to gain insight into its visible and hidden dynamics. (This topic is explored further in Chapter 6.)

Another feature of working one-to-one is the difficulty of assessing the accuracy of what our clients say about their behaviour in the workplace. What clients say can be influenced by their wish to please or impress their coach or by guilt or embarrassment at having failed to carry out an agreed action or having handled a situation badly. In some cases, clients find it difficult to give themselves enough credit and downplay what they have achieved and in others they simply lack awareness of how their behaviour is perceived by colleagues. All these factors can lead them to edit or distort their accounts, either deliberately or inadvertently. This places particular importance on our capacity to retain a critical, objective ear as we listen to our clients' accounts. We must also remember to keep an open mind about clients' colleagues whom we may hear about at length but who are not present in the coaching room. More than once over the years I have formed an impression of a client's boss or a team member based on their description only to form a significantly different impression when I meet that individual in person, perhaps at a three-way meeting or a team event.

To gain as much information as possible about how the client is really experienced at work, I use 360-degree feedback, assessment reports and other sources of external data wherever possible as well as exploring in depth the views of their line-manager and HR partner. The perceptions of the client's colleagues at all levels in the organization are invaluable. This is especially so with those clients who resist acknowledging their difficulties, underplay their strengths or convey an inaccurate picture of other people's opinions. I also draw on a range of psychometric and behavioural instruments designed to shed further light on the client's emotional and behavioural profiles. These sources of information are extremely helpful in confirming or modifying my own assessment.

Ultimately, we must hold in mind the limitations and distortions that individual work entails while leveraging its many advantages. We have to accept the subjectivity of the client's experience and the inevitable selectivity of our perceptions and remember that there is no one version of reality. It is by focusing on the individual within their wider organizational context that our work can be most effective.

Another aspect of one-to-one coaching to highlight here is that we are accountable to both the individuals we work with and to their organizations. This dual accountability is an important dimension of executive coaching, setting it apart from other kinds of coaching, as well as from psychotherapy and counselling. Managing these two relationships simultaneously adds complexity and challenge to our role. We must do our utmost to engage the individual client in the coaching process, promote their interests and respect the confidentiality boundary surrounding the sessions. At the same time, we must hold the organization's interests and needs in mind throughout and ensure that they are thoroughly addressed and evaluated. When tension exists or arises between individual and organization, we may find ourselves pulled in two directions.

Common examples of this kind of tension include the HR director who calls the coach to share negative information about the client in confidence, the client who tells the coach they have decided to leave the organization for one of its competitors but wants to keep it secret until the last moment, the line-manager who requests feedback about the client's progress to help with a promotion decision and the coach who becomes concerned that the organization is behaving unethically towards the client. In these situations, even experienced coaches can find themselves identifying too closely with the individual and losing touch with the organizational perspective. The risk then is that the coaching relationship becomes a cosy twosome, more-or-less detached from the organization that is funding the work. Similarly, coaches can also find themselves identifying too closely with the employer's perspective through close links with HR professionals or line-managers. The risk in this case is that the coaching process becomes vulnerable to inappropriate pressure on its ethics and boundaries. There is no one right answer to handling these challenges. They demand integrity and skill on the part of the coach, along with flexibility and self-awareness.

My coaching style

What I describe in this book is my own way of working. There is considerable variation in approach within the executive coaching field and no single agreed methodology. Many coaches see their task as essentially facilitating the client's progress through offering empathy and asking the right questions. They believe that it is the client's prerogative and responsibility to identify the coaching goals. They also believe that the client possesses the answers to their own problems and that the coach's role is to help draw those answers out. As the chapters that follow will show, I take a somewhat different approach.

First, I work at two levels. While engaging with the specific coaching goals identified by the individual and their organization, I may seek to reframe or modify them. I also form my own view of the client's underlying developmental goals and work to address these as well, explicitly or implicitly. Second, by drawing on the psychodynamic model and other conceptual frameworks, I aim to make sense of patterns of thinking, feeling and behaviour that lie outside the client's conscious awareness. This means that I take a proactive approach to helping clients modify unproductive patterns and establish more successful ones.

This orientation leads to my coaching style being highly interactive and quite directive at times. I go beyond providing clients with a safe space and asking skilful questions. When necessary, I lead the process, taking the initiative and directing the client towards themes, insights and behavioural changes that I believe are important. I express my opinion and, where it will help the client, I give advice. This approach has a proven track record of success and often enables me to help clients achieve a great deal in a relatively short time, with visible long-term benefits for their organizations and their own careers. However, it brings considerable responsibility. My coaching interventions are crafted with care. The pace and content of my work is sensitively tailored to the individual's needs and the way they experience me and the coaching process is always at the forefront of my mind.

Psycho-jargon has no place in any coach's vocabulary. This is particularly important for those of us who draw on psychodynamic concepts. While these ideas offer a powerful route to understanding the client, we must apply a rigorous distinction between what we think and what we say. In inexperienced or clumsy hands, there is a risk that unfiltered concepts could be formulated in a way that is highly inappropriate. This would not only damage the coaching process but could undermine the client's wellbeing if the coach's intervention was experienced as attacking or intrusive. Technical terms such as *defence mechanisms* have only two places in my practice – in my head and in discussion with my coaching supervisor or professional colleagues. They do not feature in my conversations with clients. I use clear, everyday language which builds a bridge between my view of the world and theirs.

The use of the working hypothesis

There is a further point about the way I work that is particularly important to underline. I have mentioned how the psychodynamic model provides concepts which guide my thinking and which I apply to understanding my clients' internal and external worlds. As I have indicated, I take a proactive approach and use my own judgement when identifying their characteristic psychological and behavioural patterns. Yet I am also acutely aware that I cannot know for sure whether my perceptions are correct and must regard them as possible or probable rather than certain. Through using the concept of the *working hypothesis,* I aim to strike the right balance between application of theory and keeping an open mind about what is going on for my clients as individuals and within their organizations.

I first came across the term working hypothesis in a developmental, rather than scientific, context when I became involved in the field of Group Relations in the early 1980s.[3] In this area of work, consultants attempt to decipher and explain fast-moving group dynamics use the working hypothesis to represent the version of reality that makes most sense to them at a particular time. This approach has two features which are particularly important and have led me to use it in my coaching work. First, the working hypothesis does not emerge purely as a result of theoretical assumptions but is based on *carefully observed evidence* provided by the words, non-verbal communication and behaviour of the client, and in some cases by my own responses to the client. Second, *it is not assumed to be necessarily correct* in all its aspects or even at all. Instead, the working hypothesis can and must be tested over time. As I work with my clients about whom a hypothesis has formed, I continually look for *further evidence* which will enable me to confirm, develop, amend or discard it. This seems to me to be an appropriate methodology for any developmental activity but perhaps especially so for psychodynamically influenced executive coaching. Without it, the psychodynamic approach could justifiably lay itself open to charges of being fanciful, arrogant or both.

Coaching supervision

As noted in the Introduction, I do not believe that executive coaches need to be trained in psychotherapy to draw on the psychodynamic model in their practice. The main requirement is self-awareness and maturity which can be acquired through many therapeutic and developmental routes. The capacity to empathize with others and to take an objective, analytical perspective is immensely important, along with curiosity about what lies beneath the surface of human behaviour. However, I regard excellent coaching supervision as essential if we are to work responsibly as coaches.

From my perspective, supervision should be a professional arrangement involving regular sessions with a seasoned, senior colleague where coaches can discuss their client work in strict confidence. It provides a reflective space within which specific cases can be reviewed and explored, the coach's blind spots can be identified and their skills and understanding developed over time. Its purpose is to improve the quality of the coach's work, provide a degree of quality assurance for the client, ensure a safety net for the coach when particularly complex or challenging situations arise, and raise standards in the executive coaching field. My own experience over many years as both supervisee and supervisor of other coaches has reinforced my belief in the benefits and necessity of this process.

The emotional pressure on leaders and the growth of executive coaching

The growth of executive coaching in the UK and other developed countries over the past decade has been striking. In 2009 a Chartered Institute of Personnel and Development (CIPD) survey of nearly 600 organizations across all sectors found that over 90 per cent used coaching delivered by managers or internal coaches while over 60 per cent used external executive coaches (CIPD, 2009). Even during the 2008–09 recession, there was evidence of continued recognition that investment in coaching senior individuals brings excellent returns. In my view, this growth has stemmed largely from an increasing appreciation of the difference that highly effective leadership behaviour makes to organizational performance. As this book is designed to illustrate, underpinning this behaviour is *the leader's capacity to understand and manage emotion.* When leaders fail to do this well, the impact can be destructive and far-reaching for their staff and organization as well as for themselves. However, by virtue of their role, leaders experience a set of powerful *emotional pressures* which can make this particularly difficult. These pressures include:

- **High stakes and high expectations.** Most leaders carry a strong internal sense of responsibility for their organization and their people. They are acutely aware of being accountable for important decisions that have far-reaching consequences. They often expect a great deal of themselves and suffer guilt and shame when they are unable to deliver to their own high standards.
- **Never being 'off stage'.** Leaders inevitably attract a high level of attention and commentary within their own organizations. Their behaviour, mood, body language and statements are scrutinized and speculated on by their staff. Leaders are subject to many perceptions and assumptions, positive and negative, yet must resist being too influenced by them. They must remain professional and in role – all day, every day. For those in the most senior positions, the media ensures that every aspect of their performance is closely watched and their anxiety is fuelled by the knowledge that any failures or mistakes will rapidly enter the public domain.
- **Presenting a controlled image.** Leaders are expected – by themselves and others – to be especially good at dealing with their emotions. Being effective and credible in role seems to mean controlling their feelings and hiding their doubts and vulnerabilities. This is rarely acknowledged, however, in the field of leadership education or within organizations, despite the ubiquity of the term *emotional intelligence,* first introduced to the business world by Daniel Goleman in the mid-1990s (Goleman, 1996).
- **Leading in turbulent times.** The recession of 2008–09 and the challenging economic conditions that have followed have significantly added to the demands on those in charge. The unrelenting level of change and uncertainty that has become the norm for all organizations mean that these additional demands on leaders look set to remain in place (Sandler, 2009b).

Some of these emotional pressures apply especially to those right at the top of their organizations. Yet they are also relevant to individuals at any level whose role involves taking responsibility for any aspect of performance and for leading and managing others. Although nowadays my clients are mainly business leaders and senior role-holders, over the years I have coached at all levels, in all functions and across all sectors – private, public and voluntary. This is reflected in the examples given throughout this book. Whichever kind of client and organization you work with, the range of coaching strategies and techniques that follow offer the opportunity to bring a new depth of insight and effectiveness to your practice within a safe and responsible framework. I hope that you will find something to stimulate your thinking and enhance your work.

Notes

1 360-degree feedback is a well-established process whereby a client receives anonymized feedback about their leadership from a group of typically 10–20 nominees who are a mixture of senior, peer or junior colleagues within their organization. This data is produced in the form of a report which the coach and client then go through together.
2 An increasing amount of coaching does of course take place with teams but this topic is not addressed in this book.
3 This school of thought emerged from the work of Wilfrid Bion (1897–1979) and others at the Tavistock Institute and Clinic.

2 Key concepts in psychodynamic theory

All psychodynamic models trace their roots back to Sigmund Freud (1856–1939), the founder of psychoanalysis, and his revolutionary ideas about the human mind. From his original framework, different schools of thought developed and extended his idea over the course of the twentieth century. Among the most significant contributors were Melanie Klein, Donald Winnicott and Freud's youngest daughter, Anna Freud. This process is continuing in the twenty-first century, as leading thinkers revise and develop his concepts in the light of experience and research. Yet Freud's fundamental ideas about human mental and emotional functioning remain the bedrock that underpins the psychodynamic approach.

This chapter does not provide a comprehensive or in-depth discussion of Freud's ideas, or of the development of psychodynamic theory over the past 120 years.[1] The purpose of this book is to bring the psychodynamic perspective alive in *applied form* in a *non-therapeutic context* and to demonstrate how, through skilful use, it can inform and enhance the practice of executive coaching. To this end, I have concentrated on providing a concise explanation of those key psychodynamic concepts that in my view have best stood the test of time and are widely regarded as most relevant to current thinking and practice.

The unconscious mind

Psychodynamic theory is concerned with understanding the inner world of human beings and its relationship with how we behave in the outer world and relate to other people, organizations and society. A central component of Freud's theory was the contention that we all have an unconscious as well as a conscious part of our minds. He did not consider this unconscious part simply to be the place where things that are outside our awareness are permanently stored away. Rather, he argued that we each have a 'dynamic internal world' in which there is constant interaction between conscious and unconscious thoughts, feelings, wishes, urges and fantasies. Within this inner world, the role of emotions is considered central. Pivotal to understanding the interplay between the conscious and unconscious parts of the mind is the belief that human beings have the capacity to *regulate their experience of their own emotions without being aware that they are doing so*. This means that we tend to ban from our conscious minds those unpleasant, frightening or threatening feelings that we find too difficult to tolerate.

Our defensive patterns

This process takes place unconsciously through what Freud called 'psychological defence mechanisms'. He and other psychoanalytic thinkers formulated a wide range of these mechanisms, some of which, such as *repression, denial* and *rationalization*, have become familiar expressions in everyday life. Psychodynamic theory regards these defences as a normal, helpful and indeed necessary aspect of mental functioning. Without the capacity to exclude some of our emotional experience from our conscious minds some of the time, we would be overwhelmed with anxiety and be unable to function. However, when psychological defences are used excessively, or in an immature or rigid fashion, they distort and damage our emotional wellbeing and exact a heavy price in terms of mental distress and dysfunctional behaviour. This price is paid by ourselves and by the other people with whom we interact. As an understanding of psychological defences is central to a psychodynamically oriented approach to coaching, I have illustrated several of the most common ones through client examples at the end of this chapter.

At the heart of psychodynamic theory is the belief that while all human beings use defence mechanisms to deal with difficult aspects of their internal life, individuals do not use them in either a random or universal fashion. Instead, each person's internal dynamics take shape in response to their individual experiences since birth. Our early attachments and family relationships, in particular, powerfully mould the interplay between the conscious and unconscious parts of our minds. As we grow, this results in the creation of a unique inner landscape for each individual, namely a characteristic pattern of emotions, thoughts, behaviours and defences. These patterns colour the adults that we become.

One of Freud's most important insights is that human beings have a strong unconscious tendency to retain these patterns during their lifetime, recreating over and over again the characteristic experiences of their inner world, whether they be positive or negative. Regardless of the discomfort or dysfunction they may cause, these experiences are reassuringly familiar, having been laid down early in life.

A striking example of this is when an abused child, despite suffering deeply, seeks out abusive relationships as an adult. A more everyday example is the woman whose critical mother left her feeling guilty and with low self-esteem and who, as an adult, responds in a similar fashion to a critical line-manager. Similarly, the man who grew up in a family with several siblings where parental attention was in short supply may demonstrate competitive behaviours at work to the detriment of his relationships with peer colleagues. In all these cases, the repeated pattern of behaviour – however painful or unsatisfying in practice – provides a degree of unconscious gratification and psychological safety through the powerful sense of familiarity that it provides. In addition, *these behaviour patterns also function to protect the individual against the internal conflict and anxiety that confronting their issues at a conscious level would evoke.*

It was in the context of these insights that psychoanalysis and psycho-therapy developed as clinical treatments. They were – and still are – designed to help individuals modify the unconscious patterns that have become obstacles to their emotional and psychological health.

The neurological basis of the unconscious

Although at a superficial level the notion of the unconscious mind has been widely acknowledged within our culture, in practice it is not well understood and there is considerable scepticism even within the world of psychology as to its real significance. As this concept lies at the heart of the psychodynamic approach, it is interesting to note that recent research in the field of neuroscience has revealed evidence for both the existence of unconscious functioning and for the primacy of emotional life.

Within the different systems of the human brain is the primitive limbic system, sometimes called the 'emotional brain', which contains a structure called the amygdala, two almond-shaped groups of neurons that play an essential part in decoding emotions and in particular in responding to stimuli that are threatening to us as an organism. Many sensory paths from other parts of the brain converge in the amygdala and alert it of potential dangers in the environment. As Daniel Goleman highlighted in his groundbreaking work on emotional intelligence, the amygdala plays a central but unacknowledged role in driving human behaviour (Goleman, 1996). This is because when the amygdala picks up danger signals, it instantaneously floods the body with adrenaline and other chemicals, triggering immediate anxiety and an instinctive fight, flight or freeze reaction – before we are consciously aware of what is happening.

The neocortex, our much more recently evolved 'rational brain', contains the main sites for language, the capacity to reason and to regulate emotion and behaviour. Although there is a myriad of neural pathways between the limbic brain and the neocortex, the neocortex reacts much more slowly to messages from the environment and takes much longer to process information. Experiments using sophisticated brain scanning have demonstrated that individuals react to stimuli via the amygdala – in ways that can be tracked and measured physiologically – before becoming consciously aware of them via the neocortex. This would seem to indicate the neurological basis for the existence of unconscious functioning and confirms the continuing and fundamental centrality of emotion for the human animal, despite the astonishing development and capabilities of the rational brain (Gladwell, 2006; LeDoux, 1999).

Freud's structural model of the mind

To fully appreciate the ideas about the dynamics of the mind already described, it is necessary to understand Freud's structural model, developed in 1921. In this model, he put forward a metaphorical mental framework consisting of three different components that interact with each other and create a constant two-way traffic between the conscious and unconscious parts of our minds. Although subsequent thinkers have modified significantly the way this model is seen to function, and some of the terminology is a little obscure, the essence of the structure described by Freud remains central to psychodynamic theory.

The id

The first element of the model is the *id* (the 'it' in Latin), which Freud saw as representing our most fundamental biological drives, especially the sexual and aggressive. He believed that, like other species within the animal kingdom, human beings have deep-rooted instincts that we are innately programmed to try and satisfy, regardless of the impact on others. The id is most clearly seen in action in babies and young children whose lives are dominated by their own needs, wishes and feelings. Only gradually do they learn to master their impulses, delay gratification and modify their behaviour to take other people – and social norms – into account.

The id's powerful drives do not vanish as we grow older. However, they do become increasingly hidden from view as we strive, with variable success, to control them by burying their most unacceptable aspects in the unconscious part of our minds. The particular way in which each individual handles the reservoir of biologically driven urges, desires and emotions located in the id plays a crucial role in shaping their inner world.

For Freud, this insight was central, since he believed the suffering of his patients was caused mainly by the struggle to deal appropriately with their underlying sexual and aggressive drives. Although subsequent psychodynamic theory places less emphasis on the centrality of these primal drives, the id is still seen as a significant part of mental functioning, playing as it does a crucial role in the development of the bond between children and their parents through driving the baby to attach itself to its carers and to satisfy its basic biological needs.

The ego

The second element of Freud's structural model is the *ego* (the 'I' in Latin). While colloquially the term 'ego' is used rather pejoratively as in 'we have to flatter his ego' or 'the room was full of big egos', in this model the emphasis is somewhat different. In contrast to the largely unconscious, instinct-driven id, the ego is the more conscious and rational part of the self. As a child grows older, it is the ego that engages with the everyday demands of the outside world. It is the seat of our capacity to learn, adapt, compromise, reflect, anticipate and plan, and it works hard to integrate the different parts of our emotional and cognitive selves. It is also, crucially, the source of our capacity to build successful relationships, as it is the ego that manages the ongoing balancing act between our own wishes and needs and those of other people.

It is also the ego that drives us to seek approval and praise from significant others. This is something that we all need, as children and as adults, but people vary in the degree to which they continue to need external approval throughout their adult lives, regardless of what they have objectively achieved. When the need for this sort of validation dominates an individual's personality and they tend towards self-aggrandizement, they are described as 'narcissistic'. Paradoxically, narcissistic individuals are both excessively involved with their own achievements and, consciously or unconsciously, painfully unsure of themselves. It is likely that their ego has not developed sufficiently to create a secure sense of self-esteem. This leaves them dependent on seeking an endless supply of external recognition to feel good about themselves.

A key goal is therefore the maturation of the ego. The more mature the ego, the more able we are to understand, accept and manage ourselves and to regulate our underlying drives. Crucially, a healthy ego enables us to acknowledge and tolerate painful emotions and to find appropriate ways of expressing them. This capacity to experience and express the full range of human emotions at a conscious level, rather than suppressing unpleasant feelings into our unconscious, is intimately linked to our capacity to form close attachments, understand other people's feelings and nurture and care for them. Freud believed that young children's earliest relationships with their parents were of crucial importance in the healthy development of the ego and this view remains a central tenet of psychodynamic thinking today. I shall return to this theme below.

The superego

The third element of the structural model is the *superego* ('above the I' in Latin), which Freud believed functions as our conscience, counter-balancing the expression of the id's underlying aggressive and sexual instinctual drives. Like the ego, this normally develops during early childhood as we learn to take into account other people's wishes, needs and opinions. Initially, we learn that our parents or carers expect certain types of behaviour from us and disapprove of other types of behaviour and, when young, we tend to conform to gain approval and acceptance. Over time, we develop and internalize our own version of what is right and acceptable and what is not.

People vary a good deal in how powerful and demanding a superego they develop. A weak superego results in individuals who lack a sufficient internal moral guide to prevent them from transgressing against social norms and satisfying their own needs at the expense of others. A strong superego leads to individuals who are vulnerable to being overpowered and controlled by an excessively harsh and demanding conscience. This latter group is prone to feeling easily guilty and self-critical. They tend to drive themselves – and others – extremely hard. In some cases, they suffer from a constant high level of unconscious guilt which leads to self-punishing or self-destructive behaviour and to repression of their own anger or other 'unacceptable' thoughts or feelings. In other cases, they may find their harsh superego so intolerable that they turn this voice outwards and persistently blame and attack others as well as themselves. Individuals also vary greatly in the extent to which they are consciously aware of their superego and in how successfully they are able to deal with its demands. Those with a healthier ego, whose development has supported self-awareness and self-acceptance, will be more able to recognize the superego as a powerful but manageable part of themselves and to negotiate with it to achieve a good balance between the two extremes.

Internal conflict

Thus Freud's structural model of the mind suggests that our inner worlds are propelled by powerful ongoing tensions between the different parts of the human psyche. The primal urges of the id (for example, the wish to attack hated rivals), the reality-check provided by the ego (attacking them would not be appropriate) and the self-critical inner voice of the superego (feeling guilt for wishing to attack them) interact and drive the dynamic ebb and flow of thoughts, wishes and feelings between our conscious and unconscious minds. The *internal conflicts* that these interactions create are experienced as uncomfortable at best and intolerable at worst, depending on the individual and the situation. These conflicts, conscious and unconscious, trigger anxiety, which Freud saw as an alarm call to the ego. In the face of this threat, we unconsciously mobilize psychological defence mechanisms in an attempt to resolve our emotional dilemmas and regain a sense of safety.

How individuals develop psychologically

As well as explaining how the mind is structured and the interaction of the three components, Freud's mental model suggests that human beings face several *developmental tasks* if they are to achieve mental health. These can be encapsulated as follows:

- How to channel our more primitive urges, wishes and emotions into socially acceptable forms while not losing touch with them altogether. This last point is important if we are to retain the capacity to mobilize energy, emotion and creativity.
- How to develop a moral conscience that provides us with clear guidance without being excessively critical or punitive.
- How to evolve into a balanced and resilient individual, with a positive sense of self and others, who is able to tolerate ambiguity, and sustain intimate, social and work relationships successfully.

To understand the factors determining each individual's success or otherwise in achieving these goals, we shall turn to Freud's ideas about child development. He believed that the human infant and child goes through a succession of age-related stages, each of which brings its own psychological hurdles that must be resolved in a satisfactory way if mental health is to be achieved. Although later thinkers have modified aspects of Freud's views in this area, the psychodynamic model retains at its core the view that our early life experiences – and especially our relationships with parents and other carers – have a fundamental impact on our long-term psychological health. These early experiences powerfully mould crucial aspects of the person that we become.

The psychodynamic view of child development is a huge and fascinating subject area. Here I can only highlight some of the most important dimensions and attempt to give a sense of how Freud's structural model of the mind can help to explain the significance of our early experiences.

Babies and young children, up to approximately the first two years of life, are dominated by the biologically driven and forcefully expressed instincts of the id. At this age their emotions – whether love, hate, fear or joy – are all-encompassing and, in the moment, entirely colour their attitudes towards their carers. For example, when a child of this age is angry and tells his mother that he hates her, he really means it. However, a few minutes later, when his feelings have changed and he wants to cuddle her, the loving feelings that he expresses are equally genuine. It is as if the young child experiences the mother as two people consecutively, one bad and one good. It is only gradually that he or she learns to recognize that she is one and the same person.

It is inevitable that even the most attentive and loving parent will sometimes be experienced as bad by the child and the process of learning to tolerate the frustration and disappointment this causes is a normal and important developmental milestone. It represents the early growth of the ego, which is beginning to modify and regulate the urgent demands of the id for immediate gratification.

As children become mobile and start using language, new horizons open up and they experience the excitement of discovering the world around them. Alongside this surge of curiosity and discovery, they have to cope with new experiences that are challenging and often frightening. These include learning to separate from their carers and to accept that they are not the only person at the centre of their parents' lives. Learning to share their mother with their father or another partner, to relate to siblings and other children, to be part of a group and to take turns are all part of this process, as is discovering and coming to terms with the reality of birth, illness and death. It is the child's growing ego that helps it to negotiate these tasks and to develop the vital capacity both to defer gratification and to compromise. This is accompanied by the development of the child's inner moral guide or conscience in the form of the superego. In this way, the id – which at birth propels the development of the human infant – becomes modified by the influence of the other two components of the structural model.

The importance of our early attachments

How successful this developmental process is in creating a psychologically healthy individual is believed to depend a great deal on the early environmental influences on the child. The early relationship between children and their mothers, or mother-substitutes, is held to be particularly important. The roots of this belief lie in the biological realities of the human being as a species. Human infants are unique in the extent and duration of their dependence on parents or caretakers for survival and are therefore born with a powerful innate drive to form and evoke strong bonds with significant adults. From a psychodynamic perspective, a baby's future capacity for mental and emotional health will depend on the extent to which he or she experiences the consistent presence of carers who tune in to its feelings, empathize and respond promptly and soothingly to its needs, so providing the vital conditions within which the healthy ego can grow. This kind of caretaking relationship is seen as providing much more than food, physical comfort, warmth and even affection – it also provides 'containment', a vital sense of psychological safety that enables the baby to handle the anxiety that it will experience when its needs are not immediately or perfectly met (Bion, 1962). When the baby's caretakers do not succeed in providing what the eminent psychoanalyst and child development expert Donald Winnicott (1964) called 'good enough' care, it will suffer some level of psychological and emotional disruption as the bond to the key figures in its life is compromised. For Winnicott, 'good enough' care meant, in particular, the mother's capacity to tolerate the baby's anger and neediness without being damaged or overwhelmed by it.

A relatively brief or minor disruption in the provision of good enough care, such as a temporary separation, will cause the child some anxiety and distress. However, it is when the child experiences long-term or severe rupture of the child–carer attachment that long-term consequences follow. This rupture can be caused by separation from or loss of a parent, or parental behaviour that is inadequate, ambivalent, neglectful or abusive. These situations will seriously weaken the development of the child's ego and their capacity to form and sustain close and healthy relationships will be compromised, severely damaged or destroyed.

This is why psychodynamic theory holds that the experiences in the early months and years of our lives are particularly influential in determining our long-term psychological and emotional development, with the mother–baby relationship being regarded as especially important. Other relationships, however, especially with fathers, are regarded as very important too. A good relationship with one parent, for example, can do a great deal to offset the damage caused by a poor relationship with the other. Similarly, the nature of a child's relationships with their siblings will have a powerful impact on the way in which they relate to peers later in life. Therefore, while good enough early parenting is an essential basis for mental wellbeing, events that occur later in childhood or adolescence must also be taken into account when understanding the way in which we evolve as individuals.

Neuroscience and attachment theory

Once again, modern neuroscience provides powerful confirmation of the fundamental importance of early attachment experiences on the individual's psychological and emotional development, and also about the role of anxiety in mental functioning. One of the most interesting findings concerns the force with which early experiences are imprinted on the limbic system's primitive brain. Experiments have shown that any signal from the environment that threatens separation from, loss of or rejection by the caretaking adult triggers the amygdala, the source of emotional arousal. The chemicals with which the amygdala floods the body seem to serve to imbue these earliest emotional memories – whether positive or negative – with great intensity and therefore embed them for life into the individual's brain. Despite the fact that many of these earliest emotional experiences have been shown to take place outside conscious awareness and memory, they have a critically important influence on our behaviour in adulthood (LeDoux, 1999).

Another fascinating finding is that the area of the brain that contains the capacity to relate meaningfully to others has been shown to develop only through the stimulation and sense of security a child receives from a consistent and loving carer. Research into children unfortunate enough to be deprived of this relationship, for example in the worst orphanages, not only fail to thrive, even if their physical needs are met, but also risk failing to develop the abilities needed to empathize with and love other human beings.

An illustration

To illustrate the theoretical concepts and processes explained so far, the following is an example of the unconscious dynamics of a child whose parental attachment was disrupted.

Dominic

The example concerns Dominic, a young boy whose father was prone to angry and critical outbursts towards his son. This threw the child into painful conflict. On the one hand, he felt a murderous rage against his bullying father, while on the other, he longed for his approval and felt great love and admiration for him. These mixed feelings created in Dominic a high level of anxiety. Without being consciously aware of what he was doing, he used three common psychological defences: splitting, denial and idealization. This meant that he split off the negative aspects of his father's behaviour, denied how hurtful and upsetting it was, and developed a rose-tinted view of him, exaggerating his good qualities, and blaming himself for provoking and deserving his bad temper and critical opinions. At a conscious level, this enabled Dominic to:

- preserve a positive image of his father and protected him against acknowledging the absence of the father he longed to have;
- avoid some of the pain and grief at having a father whose behaviour was harsh and rejecting;
- protect his father from the imagined effects of his own rage;
- reduce his sense of guilt at being angry with the father whom he loved, needed and longed to please, as well as hated and feared.

However, Dominic paid a heavy price for this unconscious defensive manoeuvre. His repressed feelings of hurt, grief, anger and guilt had not dissipated but remained active below the surface, in the unconscious part of his mind where they functioned as a kind of emotional toxin, distorting his psychological and emotional development in a number of ways.

In denying the pain his father caused and preserving an almost entirely good image of him, Dominic was forced to denigrate and blame himself. This created significantly low self-esteem and a weakened ego with a reduced capacity to develop a positive sense of self. He had a strong tendency to become anxious in conflict situations when his fear of his own and others' anger eroded his ability to assert himself firmly when appropriate. He also developed a highly critical superego that functioned both to internalize his father's voice, with which he had allied, and to punish him for his anger at his father as well as for the supposed failings that provoked it in the first place. As a consequence, he often withdrew from close emotional connections with others.

As an adult, Dominic struggled to fulfil his potential at work. He tended to feel excessively anxious around authority figures he experienced as prone to criticize or disapprove of him. He was also prey to unexplained episodes of depression. He married but found it difficult to communicate openly to his wife about his feelings and often expressed his dissatisfaction in passive aggressive ways such as critical remarks dressed up as jokes and sulky withdrawal. He loved his two sons but found it hard to be as close to them as he would have liked and was experienced by them as emotionally detached and critical. In these ways, Dominic, and those close to him, suffered the negative impact of his unresolved and unacknowledged feelings about his father, his unconscious defences having created psychological and emotional patterns that – without help – would continue to colour his adult life.

Psychodynamic therapy

It was in the context of the theory outlined above that Freud conceived psychoanalysis as a clinical treatment. He developed it as a technique to help patients who were suffering from all kinds of symptoms that he believed resulted from their inability to tolerate difficult and unpleasant memories, feelings and thoughts. He believed that if this unconscious material could be surfaced and understood, it would release its damaging hold on the individual's psyche. He therefore saw the role of the analyst as working to make the unconscious conscious. To this end, he encouraged the patient to say whatever came to mind and to bring their dreams to the sessions as ways of accessing unconscious material.

Freud was particularly concerned to gain access to the patient's id, as he saw the underlying instinctual drives as central to their problems. Later thinkers and clinicians have placed greater emphasis on working with the patient's ego and superego. Despite this, and other significant developments in clinical theory and practice, this essential aim of liberating individuals from negative unconscious patterns through helping them understand, experience and release unbearable thoughts and feelings remains valid for psychodynamic forms of therapy today.

Transference and counter-transference

An important aspect of the psychodynamic model that should be highlighted here is the view that the relationship between analyst and patient, or therapist and client, is of particular significance in the treatment process. Freud realized, from his early clinical work, that his patients had a tendency to relate to him in ways that seemed to have more to do with key figures from their past than with himself. This led him to believe that certain aspects of the analytic situation encouraged an unconscious transferring of the emotions involved in early relationships, positive or negative, onto the relationship with the analyst. This reflected his view that human beings have a powerful tendency to repeat early experiences throughout life without being consciously aware of what they are doing. Freud's concept of transference was extended to include the idea of counter-transference, namely the equivalent unconscious response of the analyst to the patient.

The concepts of transference and counter-transference have been considerably extended and developed over time. Most psychodynamic psychotherapists believe that we all bring to our adult relationships, both inside and outside the therapeutic setting, many of the emotional and psychological patterns of our early relationships with parents, siblings and other key figures. This is regarded as valuable information for the therapeutic work rather than a block to it. Similarly, the counter-transference is seen as comprising both conscious and unconscious elements of the therapist's own response to the client. It will reflect a mix of the therapist's own inner landscape and that of the client. The counter-transference is also seen as a valuable additional source of data about clients and how they relate to other figures in their lives. It is of course essential that the therapist is sufficiently self-aware to be able to separate his or her own contribution to the counter-transference response from that of the client.

Psychological defence mechanisms

Before exploring, in the following chapters, how the psychodynamically oriented coach can use psychodynamic theory to enhance their practice, I shall examine more fully one of the central concepts of the model. This is the way in which the unconscious mind deploys a range of *psychological defence mechanisms* to protect itself from unbearable anxiety and pain. On the one hand, as already noted, these mechanisms are part of normal human functioning. On the other hand, when the individual's early experiences have not supported the development of a healthy ego, they easily become dysfunctional. Whether they are part of the problem or part of the solution depends on how extensively and rigidly these defences are used.

Common defences include repression, denial, splitting, idealization, displacement, rationalization, intellectualization, identification, projection and projective identification. Understanding and being able to recognize when and how these defences are being used is a central part of the psychodynamic approach. The definitions below are illustrated with examples from my practice of clients who have demonstrated these defences. How I identified and addressed these defences is discussed later in the book.

Repression

This is one of the simplest – and most powerful – forms of psychological defence, involving the wholesale banning of painful or unacceptable aspects of one's experience, thoughts or feelings by pushing or keeping them deep into the unconscious part of the mind.

Nick

A coaching client who used repression was Nick. A senior HR manager, he did not feel comfortable expressing anger or resentment towards colleagues under any circumstances, even in the face of strong provocation. It was important for him to be liked, and to feel himself to be a kind and caring person and even thinking badly of other people made him feel guilty. As a result, he had pushed his aggressive feelings into the unconscious part of his mind and, at a conscious level, was genuinely convinced that they did not exist.

While repressing his aggressive side served to protect Nick from the discomfort and anxiety that acknowledging it would have evoked, this unconscious defence brought with it a cost. Although generally popular at work, Nick's colleagues would become frustrated at times with his refusal to take a firm stand on certain issues that were of concern to them. For example, when another department attempted to take all the credit for a joint project, he was seen as too understanding of their point of view and insufficiently determined to fight his own team's corner. This stance created tension in his working relationships with his colleagues, who considered him to be ineffective. Interestingly, outside work Nick was an active member of an Animal Rights pressure group and some of his repressed aggression was indirectly expressed in the strength of his indignation and fury about how animals were treated by parts of the scientific community.

Denial

This defence is similar to repression but instead of painful or threatening thoughts or feelings being entirely repressed, the individual who denies an aspect of reality often has some awareness of it, in a less conscious part of themselves, and experiences some anxiety as a result. So, typically, when an alcoholic angrily denies that their drinking is a problem, at another level they know that it is indeed a problem and one that they feel worried and ashamed about. Or, when a coaching client furiously rejects a piece of critical 360-degree feedback, their emotional reaction may indicate that below the surface the criticism has struck a chord. So denial often relates to an emotion, thought or piece of behaviour – one's own or another person's – that arises from or provokes anxiety, or intensifies the individual's inner conflict about an issue.

Belinda

Belinda, a sales manager who sought coaching to help her build confidence and impact, struggled to acknowledge her anger and distress but had not repressed these emotions in the wholesale fashion that Nick had done. In her first coaching session, she described in detail her boss's behaviour towards her. If the facts were true, his conduct amounted to serious bullying. Yet Belinda denied that the boss's behaviour was upsetting her or angering her, insisting instead that she felt sorry for him.

The coach noted, however, that her breathing became shallow, her posture tense, her voice tight and a red rash spread from her chest to her neck when she talked about what was happening, indications that she felt much more anxious and agitated than she was admitting to herself – but also that these emotions were just below the surface. By denying these feelings, Belinda was attempting to avoid the painful implications involved in acknowledging her true situation, namely that an authority figure that she had trusted was attacking her.

It also enabled her to avoid taking responsibility for doing something about it. By denying the true impact of her boss's behaviour, she could maintain her self-image as a reasonable, patient individual who could rise above this unpleasant situation with dignity and self-control. However, the price Belinda paid for her denial was a high one. As well as suffering from the physiological effects of anxiety, it made it impossible for her to mobilize herself to stand up to her boss, negotiate an alternative solution or seek help from others.

Splitting and idealization

This defence involves seeing oneself and other people in black and white terms, usually as all good or all bad, even when reality indicates otherwise.

James

I recently saw an example of *splitting* when James, a coaching client who had just started a new job, described his new boss in the most positive and glowing terms and every member of the team he had inherited in negative, critical terms. While the boss may well have been excellent and the team members lacking in many ways, it was the extreme character of both descriptions – and the early stage of these relationships – that made me feel something defensive was taking place.

This unconscious splitting functioned to help James manage the anxiety and uncertainty he felt when confronted with a difficult new role and a complex set of new relationships. Lacking self-confidence, he really wanted to have a boss whom he could look up to and depend on so there was also an element of wishful thinking here. In addition, he knew that he was expected to reduce headcount in his team and by seeing its members in negative, two-dimensional terms he protected himself from some of the pain involved in having to make people redundant. The downside of this defence of course was that he could only take truly effective decisions by seeing and acknowledging the specific combination of strengths and weaknesses in all his colleagues.

Idealization is closely associated with the defence of splitting, as it is the process of seeing another person, group or organization in excessively rose-tinted terms.

In the example above, James idealized his boss – unconsciously refusing to recognize his limitations or flaws – out of a powerful wish to have a senior figure on whose judgement he could rely entirely. Part of this dynamic emerged as a result of early life experiences in which he had depended heavily on a much-loved but dominating father who had always known the answers in any situation. The risk with idealization is not only that another person or group is not seen realistically, warts and all, but that the individual systemically underrates themselves as a result of locating all the good qualities in the idealized person.

Displacement

The defence of displacement is used when an individual directs strong but difficult feelings about a person or situation onto a different target that is easier to blame.

Giles

This defence is well illustrated by Giles, a finance manager who tended to become extremely anxious when asked to present figures to his boss's executive committee. In the run-up to these meetings, he would complain vociferously to his team colleagues about the limitations of the firm's IT system. There was some basis to his complaints about the IT system, but the timing of his outbursts, together with the emotional charge he brought to them, were good indicators that he was unconsciously displacing his difficult emotions from one thing to another. A reserved, logical individual, Giles did not feel comfortable admitting even to himself that he might be irrationally anxious or angry at being put in what felt like an exposed position by his boss. As a result of this defence, Giles lacked insight into the real cause of his experience of stress, which cut him off from exploring ways to reduce or manage it better.

Rationalization

This common defence takes the form of explaining away a difficult emotional situation. It serves to enable the individual to avoid taking responsibility for uncomfortable feelings or behaviours.

Karen

Karen, the managing director of the division of a financial services company, came to coaching as a result of critical feedback from several members of her team who experienced her management style as abrasive and at times intimidating. Karen's initial response to this painful feedback was to rationalize why her colleagues might have said these things, citing factors that lay entirely outside her control. Primarily, she argued, the people who had complained were unhappy because they were longstanding members of staff who would object to any MD who tried to modernize the company. The way in which she had gone about modernizing it was not relevant, she argued. She also claimed that they were blaming her for a pay freeze imposed by Head Office, simply to express their dissatisfaction. While there was an element of truth in Karen's arguments, they entirely discounted her own contribution to the situation and the extent to which the negative feedback was the result of her own behaviour.

Intellectualization

Often confused with rationalization, this defence is more subtle. It appears as if the individual using this defence is engaging with an issue but in fact this engagement is at a purely intellectual, abstract level and functions as an alternative to taking action.

Lawrence

A coaching client called Lawrence was put in charge of a change management project. We discussed what action he could take to help staff members who were struggling with anxieties and negative feelings about the change. Whenever we broached this topic, Lawrence would agree that it was important but would somehow never be willing to focus on practical steps. Instead, he would talk animatedly but at a general, theoretical level about the issue, telling me about several books that he had read on the subject, comparing three different change management models and so on. It is likely that Lawrence's unacknowledged emotional discomfort around the question of staff anxiety was driving this defence, which functioned to keep his feelings at arm's length. Unfortunately, it was also functioning to block him from taking appropriate action to help his staff.

Identification

As young children, part of our development naturally includes wishing to be like our parents, particularly the parent of the same gender. They are our role models as well as having a central part in caring for us and helping us learn and grow. Seeing oneself as becoming like them also helps us to cope with our sense of relative weakness and immaturity compared with the adult parent's strength and competence. Identification can also function as a defence against uncomfortable feelings, however, when it is used in an excessive or inappropriate way.

Peter

A successful entrepreneur, Peter had been brought up by a father who did well in business but had been a failure in school and had become negative about academic learning and in particular people who had been to university. Peter, too, had struggled at school as a result of dyslexia that was diagnosed only later in life (and which had most likely also affected his father) and this had led to feelings of low self-esteem, frustration and shame. One of the ways in which he coped with these painful emotions was to identify not only with his father's similarly painful experience but also with his rather extreme views. While at one level this strong identification helped to shore up his self-esteem, at another level it interfered with Peter's ability to perceive the damaging consequences of his father's attitudes and to develop his own, more balanced and constructive viewpoint.

Projection

This common defence mechanism takes place when we unconsciously export an aspect of ourselves that we are not able to tolerate consciously to another person or group, and then blame or criticize them for the fault. We are all prone to using projection in everyday life but those individuals who have low self-awareness and an intolerant inner voice or superego tend to use projection a great deal, even in the face of evidence indicating that the other person does not fit the projection.

Julia

Julia, who worked as an executive in a well-known publishing house, was a good example of this. As the third of four girls in a family where her parents longed for a boy, she had grown up feeling overlooked and insufficiently acknowledged. In adult life, she had become a highly competitive individual who was critical of others – yet her punitive superego led to her feeling guilty about these aspects of herself. As a result, she unconsciously disowned them, projecting them onto her colleagues and experiencing them as unfailingly competitive and critical instead. In coaching, she described in a plausible fashion the behaviour of her boss and a peer as deplorably underhand and aggressive towards her. It was only over time, when this pattern was repeated, that the coach realized the extent of the projection and was able to help Julia begin to acknowledge and tolerate the competitive and critical parts of herself and to see others more realistically.

Projective identification

The final defence mechanism I shall outline here is projective identification. It is similar to projection in that it involves exporting unwanted or intolerable feelings into another person. However, there is an important difference which is best explained via an example.

Charlie

A good instance of this defence in action arose when I was supervising another coach. My colleague was an experienced coach who usually felt quite confident in her role. However, when she had started working with a recently promoted public sector manager called Charlie, she found herself feeling inadequate and deskilled: 'It seems as if nothing I do is helpful. He has not expressed dissatisfaction with the coaching – in fact he seems quite positive – but I have this sense of not being good enough and not knowing how to move forward. I leave the sessions feeling rather useless.'

As we explored Charlie's character and the issues he was facing, we both realized that he was likely to be feeling quite insecure in his new, more senior role. He was not the first choice for this job and it had been offered only after an external candidate decided not to take it. His new boss was not particularly supportive of Charlie and was giving him little positive feedback. Although clues to this had emerged in the coaching sessions, Charlie had not expressed any of this explicitly to his coach. Instead, he had maintained that everything was more or less fine and insisted that he was coping well. On reflection, the coach felt that these assertions lacked conviction.

We hypothesized that Charlie may unconsciously have been using projective identification to defend himself against the anxiety and insecurity that he was experiencing at work. Rather than simply projecting his sense of inadequacy onto the coach, and then criticizing her, he was *evoking in her those feelings of inadequacy*. This was achieved through subtle unconscious behaviour, for example through not acknowledging the value of any of her comments or suggestions. Therefore, the coach's uncharacteristic feelings of uselessness were the result of an unconscious communication from the client, via the mechanism of projective identification, of how he was actually feeling himself. Once the coach realized this, her sense of being deskilled disappeared and we were able to discuss how she might address Charlie's insecurity.

Applying the psychodynamic model

In this chapter, I have introduced the underlying framework of the psychodynamic model. My aim has been to make the key concepts as coherent and accessible as possible. Some of you will be interested in deepening your understanding of the theory. Others will be primarily concerned with the application of these ideas in a coaching context. In the following chapters, I shall build the bridge between concepts and practice.

Note

1. All Freud's ideas can be found in the *Standard Edition* of his *Complete Works* edited by J. Strachey *et al.* (1953–1974) and in a wealth of books that provide a good introduction to the subject. See the Bibliography.

3   Understanding the client

This chapter begins the process of linking psychodynamic theory and executive coaching practice. It focuses on the task of *understanding the client* – making sense of their thoughts, emotions and behaviour. Through supervising other coaches, I have found that this crucial stage of coaching is often underestimated, or rushed through, in favour of saying or doing something to help the client. This is perhaps not surprising given the pressure of a fixed-period coaching programme. Yet it is only by taking the time to understand what is going on that we are able to shape the most appropriate and effective interventions.

Key assumptions drawn from the psychodynamic model

Below I present the key assumptions that I have drawn from the psychodynamic model and which I use to guide my work. They form a bridge between the theoretical concepts and the application of insight to coaching clients. Each assumption is illustrated with case material that demonstrates their implications for my coaching practice.

Assumption 1: The client has unconscious thoughts and feelings

This first assumption is a fundamental one that underpins all the others. It is that all human beings at times experience thoughts, urges and emotions too painful, threatening or uncomfortable to be admitted into conscious aware-ness. Instead, they are consigned to the unconscious parts of our minds. This phenomenon is a double-edged sword. It represents a useful protective strategy for the individual but can also be the source of unhelpful symptoms, as the unconscious thoughts and feelings may continue invisibly to bubble away, causing varying degrees of mischief. What are the implications of this assump-tion for my practice?

The first implication for my practice is that when I gather data about the client, I retain a slightly detached, observing part of my mind, which assesses the client at the same time as engaging warmly in the relationship. I pay attention to many different sources of information, noting what clients choose to share and what not to share, how they use language and the tone and range of their voice. I observe their face, eye contact, breathing, posture, appearance, behaviour and general presence. I become particularly alert to the possibility of unconscious dynamics when I notice any contradictions between what the client is saying, their non-verbal communication and how they are behaving. In such situations, the words might be clear but the other signs might be indicating something different that is going on below the surface.

A good example of this is the client who insists that they are committed to the coaching process and keen to engage yet repeatedly cancels sessions or arrives late. At a conscious level the client may see these problems as due entirely to external circumstances. While not discounting the role of external reality, my hypothesis would be that there is a part of them that feels quite ambivalent about the coaching and is being expressed unconsciously through deeds not words.

The second implication is that, from the outset of coaching, I retain a particularly open mind as to what the client's issues and difficulties might be. I listen carefully to their narrative but do *not automatically accept at face value their version of reality*. While accepting their sincerity, I also respect my own responses and thoughts. I know that my perceptions of the client will almost certainly be to some extent different to their own view of themselves.

Nick

A clear example of unconscious dynamics that illustrates this point emerged in the work with Nick, the HR manager we met in the previous chapter who tended to repress his aggression. In describing his difficult relationship with a female direct report, he outlined several incidents in which he had talked to her about her performance, which was patchy, and she had become highly defensive and critical of him. This had come to a head during her annual appraisal meeting where she had attacked Nick for 'setting her up to fail' and then burst into tears. When I dug deeper and asked Nick for the facts, it seemed clear that he had in fact done a good deal to support – and indeed coach – this team member who had a record of failing to complete tasks on time, being emotionally volatile and taking frequent time off for stress-related ailments. The picture that emerged was one of a young woman whose performance was poor and whose behaviour was inappropriate and manipulative. Nick, however, blamed himself. He insisted that he should have done more to help her and argued that her failure and distress reflected poor management on his part.

To my mind, this version of events simply did not add up. Even if he could have done more or handled her better, this would not have justified her behaviour. I had already noted other evidence of Nick's tendency to belittle his own abilities, his clear discomfort with situations involving conflict and his strong wish to have a positive view of other people. I therefore developed a working hypothesis that Nick was unconsciously distorting his judgement of both his team member's behaviour and his own. Without being aware of it, he seemed to have consigned his anger with her to the unconscious part of his mind. Instead, he focused on criticizing his own behaviour *to avoid acknowledging the extent of his colleague's weaknesses and her passive aggressive behaviour towards him.*

The pay-off for this strategy was clear – Nick protected himself in the short term from the anxiety he would feel if he allowed himself to see his direct report's behaviour for what it really was; not only would this have been uncomfortable for him, it would have raised the need for him to address the situation more firmly. However, the penalty of this strategy for Nick was apparent in the form of lowered self-esteem, reduced credibility in the eyes of his other team members and a failure to hold this under-performing individual to account.

Edward

Another example of unconscious behaviour relates to a client called Edward. He was a successful operations manager who found public speaking difficult. When I saw him a few days before an important presentation, he insisted that he was feeling absolutely fine about it. However, as we discussed it, I noticed an angry-looking red rash gradually appear on his neck. He also mentioned in passing that he had not been able to sleep well for the past couple of nights but attributed this to his wife having been restless due to a slight cold. He remained convinced that he was not going to experience his usual intense anxiety about the presentation. However, the day before the event, these feelings crowded back and were overwhelming. Fortunately, his HR colleague, to whom he was close, was able to give him emergency support and in the end the presentation went well. In my view, he had been denying his anxiety in an unconscious attempt to keep control and avoid his usual pre-presentation crisis; ultimately this was not a strategy that had served him well. The severe nature of the last-minute crisis that broke through his defences left him considerably shaken; he also had much less time to face and master his fears before going on-stage.

The third implication for my practice is that, during and after coaching sessions, I tune into my own unfiltered mental, emotional and physical response to the client and their material and use this as potentially an additional and valuable source of information.

In Edward's case, for instance, in the session where he was insisting that he felt fine, I found myself feeling physical anxiety in the form of a slight pain in my stomach and a sense of tightness in my throat and chest. While this may partly have been an empathic response to the client's situation, its unusual intensity – and experience of my reactions in similar situations – made me feel that I was also picking up the high level of anxiety that Edward was suppressing. This significantly added to my hypothesis that he was in denial, despite insisting that he felt fine. Unfortunately, this was not something that I was able to help him surface in this session.

Assumption 2: The client's emotional experiences are of central significance

The psychodynamic model places particular emphasis on the central role of emotion in human experience. Not only are emotional reactions neurologically linked to the most fundamental part of our brains but our early emotional experiences as a baby and child are critical factors in how we develop. As adults, emotion remains a central driver of our opinions, attitudes and behaviour, whether we are aware of this or not. For our coaching clients, the normal ups and downs of working life inevitably arouse strong feelings, and arouse them much more easily than is usually supposed. This is true for the most rational and unemotional among them, including those in the highest positions of responsibility.

In approaching my work, I assume not only that emotion is central to all of us but that each of us has a characteristic pattern of emotional responses and that these patterns have developed as a result of the combination of our life experiences and our innate temperaments. Identifying the client's characteristic emotional pattern is at the heart of my coaching, as it paves the way to addressing those aspects that need to change.

Understanding a client's emotional life and recognizing these patterns is not always easy, however. As human beings, we often find it painful, uncomfortable or embarrassing to acknowledge apparently irrational feelings such as anxiety, fear, anger, resentment, envy, shame or guilt. In our culture especially, the same discomfort may also apply to acknowledging more positive feelings such as pride and pleasure in our own achievements. Showing their feelings, or even admitting their feelings to themselves, equates with vulnerability for many people. While clients are sometimes fully or partly aware of their feelings but keep them hidden from others, including the coach, at other times these feelings exist only at an unconscious level. For these reasons, our clients' emotions are often invisible drivers – we see the results in terms of what they say and do but often in disguised or distorted form.

Given the importance of understanding the client's feelings, and despite these difficulties, when I supervise other coaches I often suggest that they *look for the emotion*. Within the plethora of themes and topics that clients may bring to a session, this should guide the decision about what to focus on first. In my experience, the *hot* issue for a coaching client, whether or not they are consciously aware of it, is the one around which they currently have the strongest feelings. If this is not addressed, the coaching conversation risks taking place purely on the surface while the really important question – the one preoccupying the client, consciously or unconsciously, below the surface – will go unaddressed.

To help the process of looking and listening for my clients' emotional experience, I find it useful to consider the following questions:

- How wide does this client's emotional range appear to be?
- How fully do they articulate or otherwise share their feelings with me or others?
- What kind of positive feelings do they most readily express? Excitement, pride, triumph, gratitude, affection?
- What kind of negative feelings do they most readily express? Anger with others, anger with themselves, anxiety, guilt, sadness, shame?
- How aware are they of the impact of their emotions on their attitudes and behaviours?
- How skilfully do they handle their feelings at work, normally and when they are under particular pressure?
- How well do they manage different working relationships?
- How might the client be feeling about me and the coaching process?

Eva

A good example of a client whose feelings were well hidden but crucial to the coaching process is a young woman who had decided to pay for coaching herself, following redundancy from an investment bank. She approached a colleague of mine and explained that she wanted to use coaching to help her make a decision between three or four possible options regarding the next stage of her career. She was keen to use the sessions to analyse the pros and cons of staying in the investment banking sector, starting her own business, doing an MBA or returning to work in her father's manufacturing business where she had worked for 18 months in her early twenties. This sounded like a reasonable proposition, with the coach providing a sounding board and helping the client to structure her thinking and evaluate these different paths.

It soon became clear, however, that something odd was happening. Despite animated and apparently productive discussions taking place in the sessions, none of the action points the client agreed to take – for example, information-gathering activities and networking meetings – were being followed through. The coach also had the growing feeling that the conversations themselves were simply going round and round and the client seemed to be getting no nearer to a decision. It was only when the coach, having been to supervision, decided to focus in much greater depth on the client's feelings about her family business and working for her father that the real coaching issue emerged.

It turned out, as is often the case for the grown children of successful entrepreneurs, that the client had a number of painful and contradictory feelings about this subject, including anger, sadness, fear, guilt and shame. She found her father controlling and deeply resented his domineering approach. Part of her wanted to continue to keep her distance but she also loved and admired him and wanted to make him proud. She had hoped to show him that she could succeed on her own account in the tough world of investment banking; she felt shame and failure at having lost her job. In addition, she knew that he wanted her to return to the business and felt bad about having stayed away. He was offering her a senior role in the company that could lead to the opportunity to succeed him as CEO one day; to walk away from that meant possibly walking away from her birthright and the fortune that would go with it. It was only when the coach made it possible for her to connect with all these feelings and explore them openly that she began to engage authentically in the coaching process and the real work of exploring and clarifying her feelings could begin, leading ultimately to a clear career decision.

Roger

Another good example of the need to focus on the nuance of the client's emotional experience was Roger, the financial controller in a large corporate business, who came into coaching with me after learning that an outside hire was going to succeed his boss when the latter retired, despite indications over several years that he was the favoured successor. Roger was offered coaching by his organization in recognition of his disappointment, to help him consider his career options within the company and to work on his development areas, particularly his influencing skills.

Roger, like many finance professionals, was a logical, task-oriented individual and in the early stages of coaching he played down the impact of not getting the expected promotion. As well as denying feeling angry with members of senior management, he didn't find it easy to share any other feelings about what had happened. From carefully observing Roger's voice and body language and noting my own responses to his narrative, I sensed a sterile, restrained quality in what this client was telling me. I began to feel sure that his feelings about what had happened were much more powerful than he was able or willing to recognize.

Through carefully exploring this theme, it emerged that Roger was indeed angry with his retiring boss and other senior managers whom he felt had betrayed him. He was also furious with himself for having been foolish enough to believe their half-promises. However, the most painful emotion that he was experiencing – and the one that he found the hardest to admit – was not anger but *shame*. It turned out that he felt exposed and humiliated in the eyes of his finance team and other colleagues, all of whom had known about his failure to secure the expected promotion. Through the coaching process, Roger was gradually able to accept how he really felt about what had happened, to process those feelings and to mourn the loss of his hopes and vision for his future. It was only then that he could begin to engage in considering his next career step and invest energy in exploring his development needs.

Assumption 3: Understanding anxiety is particularly important

I believe that emotion in general – and *anxiety* in particular – plays a much greater role in our lives, and the lives of our clients, than is generally acknowledged or understood. At a theoretical level, Freud saw anxiety as a signal to the ego of a potential threat. These signals are received physiologically by the amygdala, which resides in our ancient limbic brain, and which responds with an instantaneous release of adrenaline and other chemicals. While on the one hand this anxiety response continues to play a vital and appropriate role in alerting us to risk or danger, on the other it leaves the highly evolved, more rational animals we have become with a good deal of undischarged tension and discomfort. In my experience, this is true for all of us to some extent, including those individuals whose early care was emotionally good enough, whose attachments were not significantly disrupted and whose developmental influences were largely positive. The concept of psychological safety helps to understand this. As explained in Chapter 2, this is a fundamental human need that is expressed, from birth, as an underlying urge to find and retain a basic sense of physical, psychological and emotional security.

These assumptions about the role of anxiety mean that I bring to my practice an acute awareness of the speed and extent with which our clients become anxious when faced with a wide range of work-related situations. *In particular, this is true of situations involving change, uncertainty, real or threatened loss and the risk of criticism, rejection or failure* – all of which characterize working life in the twenty-first century, perhaps especially for those in positions of responsibility.

The role of anxiety can be seen particularly clearly at the outset of the coaching process when it unconsciously drives some clients to demonstrate an exaggerated version of their usual defences.

Geoff

For example a new client called Geoff, a business development manager in a large insurance company, was extremely self-critical during our first meeting, underplaying his strengths, emphasizing his weaknesses and repeatedly making jokes at his own expense. While he turned out to have an underlying tendency to behave in an excessively self-deprecating way, this was clearly exacerbated by anxiety and an unconscious form of defence against his fear of my criticism.

Luisa

Another example was Luisa, a young Brazilian entrepreneur co-leading a successful medium-sized enterprise. In her case, at our first meeting, she simply did not stop talking. It was practically impossible for me to say more than a word or two before she interrupted. Naturally talkative anyway, on this occasion she produced a flood of words that I felt was unconsciously designed to dominate and neutralize me as well as cover up her anxiety at being scrutinized by a coach.

Max

Similarly, a client called Max, who ran a small but highly successful international charity, spent much of our first session together telling me about his achievements, awards and dropping the names of the famous people he knew. Again, this turned out to be a characteristic strategy that he used to boost his low self-esteem but it was particularly marked under the pressure of his anxiety during this initial meeting.

As these examples demonstrate, one critical reason that the role of anxiety is so easily overlooked in coaching is that it is frequently entirely or partially outside the client's conscious awareness and therefore *manifests itself in behaviour that does not appear on the surface to have any link with anxiety at all*. Asking what role anxiety might be playing is one of the most frequent and fruitful questions I consider in the course of working out what might lie behind my clients' thoughts, feelings and behaviour.

Finally, I shall illustrate the impact that anxiety has for some clients as they engage with their organizational tasks.

Ruth

Ruth was a senior accountant within a large regional firm. Following promotion to the role of head of department, she was offered coaching to provide her with focused support in dealing with an expanded workload and additional people management responsibilities. A hardworking, committed and valued member of the organization, at her first coaching session Ruth appeared tired and harassed. She seemed burdened rather than delighted by her promotion to her new role. It soon emerged that she was finding it extremely difficult to prioritize between tasks, to delegate sufficiently to her colleagues or to accept that some of her old activities simply could not be fitted in alongside her new ones. She seemed to feel responsible for everything and was working unsustainably long hours at the expense of her health.

It became clear to me that this problem went far beyond poor time management or a lack of delegation skills – Ruth had been trained in these areas and knew what to do, at least in theory. It was more a case of her being extremely resistant to letting go of anything; and the more tired and pressured she became, the more she persisted in trying to control everything. Her usual courteous and reasonable demeanour with colleagues was also suffering as she displayed unusual levels of irritation in her attempts to get through an unrealistic list of tasks.

It was only through exploring in some depth Ruth's underlying emotional experience that we were able to gain a clearer picture of what was going on. Essentially, she was feeling intensely anxious about failing in her new role and, in particular, about letting down her managing partner to whom she felt great loyalty and who had been the driving force behind her appointment as head of department. This feeling, in turn, was linked to experiences within her family where her parents had continually emphasized the importance of delivering on one's promises. Gradually, Ruth was able to understand how anxious she became in the face of a mounting number of tasks and how her strategy for dealing with this – keeping control of everything and trying to do it all herself – was not serving her or her firm well. Having explored the dynamics that were driving her, Ruth gradually became able to acknowledge the anxious feelings and to separate them from her behaviour. With this insight came the possibility of managing her workload in a more realistic and effective way.

Assumption 4: Clients often experience internal conflict

Closely related to understanding our clients' hidden anxiety is the importance of holding in mind the idea of *internal conflict*. This psychodynamic concept suggests that human beings regularly experience a psychological and emotional clash, at an unconscious or a conscious level, between contradictory sets of wishes, thoughts and feelings. Moreover, it seems that we find the experience of internal conflict a particularly uncomfortable one.

These conflicts often trigger unconscious anxiety, which in turn leads the individual to deploy one or more psychological defence mechanisms in an attempt to retain a sense of psychological safety. Psychodynamic theory argues that some inner conflict takes place when our urges to gratify our basic biological instincts – sexual, aggressive, territorial – conflict with the demands of our conscience and of society.

For example, an executive might feel both the urge to dominate and win within a competitive work situation and also the wish to behave considerately towards others and be liked.

Erik

Erik, a Dutch client I worked with some years ago, illustrates this point well. He was a classic alpha male in a senior role within his company, responsible for the performance of one of its main divisions in Europe. He had many strengths but the downside of his undoubted force of character, talent and determination was his tendency to be extremely competitive with his peers and senior colleagues. They experienced him as robust at best, and dominating and aggressive at worst. Although feedback to this effect had failed to bring about much change, colleagues acknowledged that Erik did usually recognize when he had gone too far and would apologize to any individuals he had particularly offended.

As Erik reached forty, he began fully to recognize the difficulties that his aggressively territorial approach was causing and he sought coaching to address this issue. It soon became apparent that there was a part of Erik that was capable of empathy and was well attuned to how others might experience him. He emphasized that he did not set out to upset or offend his colleagues. In fact, he was really upset at the idea that people sometimes considered him a bully, insisting, 'I hate bullying and would never do that – I just feel passionate about doing the right thing for my part of the business!' It seemed clear to me that Erik had a genuine internal conflict between his underlying urge to get his own way and be the dominant male and another part of himself that recognized the impact on others and wished to behave in a more considerate and acceptable way. Up until then, he had resolved this conflict by rationalizing his behaviour – maintaining that it was the right thing to do for his division and necessary, in any case, in a dog-eat-dog world. Over the course of the coaching process, Erik explored in some depth his inner conflict. This process enabled him to make a more conscious and reflective choice about how to behave and he went on to moderate his style very constructively, without losing his passion and drive.

Internal conflict does not always involve our biological urges battling with our conscience. It also exists in the form of tension between any two sets of thoughts and emotions experienced by an individual in relation to a particular issue or situation. These conflicts are regularly evoked in the course of everyday life. After all, every change, however positive, brings with it some feelings of loss; every decision or choice brings with it some level of risk and uncertainty. Being fully in touch with contrasting feelings about something seems to be both inevitable and difficult. What we call 'mixed feelings' can often represent a significant inner conflict that generates anxiety too uncomfortable to tolerate. As a result, psychological defences are unconsciously used to resolve them.

> *Ruth*
> A final example of internal conflict comes from Ruth, whose hidden anxiety was described earlier. In her case, the tension she felt was between a rational recognition of the need to prioritize and delegate and an emotional resistance to letting go of any of her work. Intellectually, she entirely understood the good reasons for creating a more manageable workload and the negative consequences for all concerned if she did not. In contrast, a less conscious but powerful part of herself became extremely anxious at the thought of relinquishing control over her work in any way. She found it almost impossible to tolerate emotionally the risk of not delivering in every area and of letting people down. It was through framing and surfacing this conflict in the course of coaching that Ruth was gradually able to acknowledge the invisible obstacle that was preventing her behaviour from matching her logical thoughts.

When coaching, I do my best to identify what issues seem to arouse particular internal conflict in the client and what form this conflict takes, how aware they are of their mixed feelings, and how they respond to and manage them. This provides invaluable information about areas they will need to develop to become more effective at work.

Assumption 5: The client will have developed an embedded characteristic defensive pattern for dealing with difficult emotions and internal conflicts

I hope it is becoming clear that the dynamics described above – the presence of unconscious as well as conscious thoughts and feelings, the centrality of emotions and anxiety in particular, the tension caused by internal conflict and the search for psychological safety – are part of normal mental functioning. I assume that I shall observe them in all my clients. However, human beings do not experience or demonstrate these dynamics in a random or constantly changing fashion. Each of us develops our own typical and enduring emotional, psychological and behavioural patterns that build on the innate aspects of our personalities. These patterns both reflect and mould our characters, making us who we are. For many people, the strategies and patterns they develop for dealing with life are less than successful.

Yet human beings find these patterns extremely difficult to change and we tend to repeat them, even when they are not serving us well.

To understand our clients' characteristic patterns of functioning and what underlies them, we need to focus particularly closely on the concept of *psychological defence mechanisms* introduced in Chapter 2. The psychodynamic model argues that all human beings use these defences as a normal part of everyday mental functioning. If we did not, we would be overwhelmed by anxiety and other painful emotions. However, the defences that help us feel safe and negotiate life's difficult experiences can also form the obstacles that hinder us from realizing our potential. Even more importantly, many people suffer varying degrees of emotional, mental and sometimes physical pain as a result of using defences in an excessive or rigid way. Therefore, as a psychodynamically oriented coach I regard it as both normal and inevitable that clients will use psychological defences to protect themselves against painful and threatening thoughts and feelings. To help them meet their goals, I seek to identify the defences they use most often.

Gerald

To illustrate how one client used defence mechanisms, let us turn to Gerald, who demonstrated a habitual pattern of unconscious strategies designed to keep at bay the feelings that emerged when he felt responsible for a mistake or misjudgement. These defences emerged particularly clearly in the course of one session. On this occasion, Gerald arrived at my office in an agitated state. Almost before he had sat down he launched into a long and angry description of his boss's unreasonable behaviour. Listening carefully, I gathered that the boss's 'crime' – not being firm enough with a difficult peer colleague – was not a new problem but something we had already explored on more than one occasion. In this context, Gerald's strength of feeling struck me as out of proportion to the apparent cause. I asked myself whether he might be using *displacement* – namely, directing his agitated and angry feelings at the easy target of his boss's behaviour while the true origin of these feelings might lie at least partly elsewhere.

When I steered the conversation towards other areas of possible emotional significance for Gerald, it quickly emerged that there was a more authentic source of agitation for him. This was the lacklustre performance, at an important recent meeting, of his newly appointed financial controller. Gerald initially dismissed it as 'just teething troubles' but this felt like *denial* to me as I knew how important this new hire's performance was for him. When I gently suggested that this poor performance might have been disappointing, Gerald admitted that it was and it emerged that he was in fact feeling both disappointment and anger with his new team member who had not prepared properly and had let him down.

Gerald's discomfort with these feelings was clear, however, and he then attempted to use *rationalization* to push them away. He disowned his anger and insisted that it was unreasonable as many people would perform poorly at their first important meeting, due to the pressure, and that his new controller had probably been tired from moving house and had not had enough time to prepare. These facts may have been correct but what made Gerald's comments feel to me like rationalizations was their timing – immediately after he had briefly acknowledged his anger and disappointment – and their purpose, which was to soothe himself by distancing himself from these uncomfortable emotions.

What other defences had Gerald demonstrated in this session? At the outset, he was aware of being angry but had related this only to his boss and had denied his anger with the new financial controller. Unconsciously, he was also avoiding his anger with himself at not ensuring that the new hire was properly prepared, possibly some guilt at not having helped him prepare and certainly some shame at having his new financial controller perform poorly in front of his boss and other colleagues. He also felt anxious at the thought that he had possibly made a poor recruitment decision in choosing this financial controller.

Gerald was also using the defence of *projection* by criticizing his boss's weakness in confronting a poor performer. This was an area that he himself struggled with, as the situation with the financial controller underlined, yet it was too painful for him to tolerate this awareness. He therefore unconsciously exported this fault to his boss and attacked it. In this way, he avoided the pain of confronting his own failings in relation to his new hire.

In working with Gerald over time, it became clear that the combination of displacement, rationalization, denial and projection were part of a *characteristic pattern* of unconscious behaviour designed to protect himself against the shame and loss of self-esteem he experienced when he had made a mistake or taken a poor decision.

Assumption 6: Clients' early family relationships and life experience play an important part in the development of their characteristic patterns

So how does the individual's *characteristic pattern* develop? Why do human beings continue to repeat patterns that do not serve them well? As outlined in Chapter 2, the psychodynamic model regards our early life experiences as particularly important in establishing our emotional and behavioural patterns. When I meet my coaching clients I assume that, like the rest of us, they will have been heavily influenced by their family background and early development. They will also reflect the impact of their educational, social, cultural and career-related experiences as well as their innate personality type and temperament.

As an executive coach, my focus is primarily on the way in which the clients' patterns affect their current working life and it does not feel appropriate to explore their early life or childhood experiences in depth. However, with most of my clients there will be a point in the coaching process at which I ask about their background. In some cases this is at the outset of the coaching process, in others it is much later on or not at all. A great deal depends on the individual and their willingness to bring this material to coaching, and on their specific issues.

Though not essential, it can be particularly useful to gain a sense of a client's parental role models, their relationships with siblings, their social patterns during adolescence and on occasion other formative influences in their childhood and adolescence. This information can provide helpful clues to understanding how they deal with pressure and anxiety and how they relate to bosses, peers and junior colleagues at work.

Deirdre

For example, a client called Deirdre came to coaching to help adapt her management style. She knew that she needed to become more inclusive and less dominating, and acknowledged that she became easily irritated if she felt that her ways of doing things were being challenged by her subordinates. In exploring why this triggered her anger, it emerged that she had a domineering mother and a passive father. Her mother was an angry and intolerant woman and her father had learned not to argue with his wife, as she would explode if he questioned her.

Not surprisingly, this family dynamic had a powerful effect on this client's development. On one level, she had clearly identified with her mother's behaviour, seeing her as strong and powerful. If her own behaviour was challenged, she tended to become defensive, blaming others for making her bossiness necessary. On another level, she had also empathized with her father's humiliation at her mother's hands and felt guilty about not supporting him more actively. This led her to be uncomfortable with this aspect of her behaviour, to realize that it upset others and to wish that she was liked more and feared less at work. She also recognized that it was career-limiting.

In the case of Deirdre, exploring the parental behaviour that she grew up with proved immensely helpful to the coaching process. It enabled her to make the links between her own behaviour and her parental role models. This deepened her insight and strengthened her wish to make some changes in how she related to her colleagues.

Yet with other clients I coach, their background or family of origin may barely appear in the course of the work. This usually applies to individuals who are not comfortable in looking at this material but it also applies to clients with whom I have found it possible to make good progress through working purely with how they function in the workplace and in the 'here and now' of the coaching sessions.

Crucially, when a client's family background or aspects of their personal life *are* explored during the coaching process, as opposed to in a therapeutic setting, the purpose is always to help us achieve their work-related objectives. So, although I might usefully discuss with a client her ferocious rivalry with her younger sister, the insights we gain are always applied to the relevant coaching issue, in this instance how she could handle her relationships with certain peer colleagues more effectively.

Assumption 7: The coach–client relationship is an important source of insight and an agent of change

This assumption comes from the psychodynamic concepts of transference and counter-transference and the belief that human beings tend unconsciously to recreate, or transfer, past relationships with parents, siblings and others to relationships with significant figures in the present. As a result, the relationship between professional practitioner and client is regarded as particularly important. This applies primarily to the psychotherapeutic setting but is also highly relevant to the practice of executive coaching. In addition, I believe that the coach–client relationship itself is a central factor in helping the client to develop and change (this theme is explored in Chapter 4).

There are many ways in which understanding transference and counter-transference helps to shed light on my clients' characteristic psychological and emotional patterns. This is especially so at the outset of the coaching process when the client's transference is often most evident.

David

David is an example. He arrived at our first meeting exactly on time. He started our conversation by thanking me for making the time to see him and telling me how impressed he had been by my biography and how his boss, who had recommended me, held me in high esteem. As we began to explore his work role and some of his coaching issues, I found that more or less whatever I said met with instant agreement from David, who responded with positive comments such as 'That's absolutely spot-on' and 'You're so insightful!' While it is always a little tempting to bask in the glow of a client's admiration, I was well aware that David's behaviour was reflecting something important about him rather than me. He was clearly using *idealization*, possibly as a defence against feeling disappointed or angry with me, but his behaviour was so marked that I felt it represented something more. I wondered whether he was transferring to me something from a past relationship – perhaps the assumption that I was a potentially threatening or critical authority figure who must be flattered and appeased.

As I learned more about David, it emerged that his mother had been a difficult, narcissistic woman who needed a constant supply of admiration and compliments to remain in a good mood. It became clear that he had tended to adopt the same approach with older female colleagues, in particular, as he had with me. His transference had opened up a fruitful theme that we were able to examine in due course, with a view to helping David modify this pattern.

Max

I have also found that my counter-transference to the client can be especially instructive at the start of the process when I am responding to first impressions. Max, the client mentioned already who showed off and name-dropped in his first session is a good example of this. Although I was aware that his behaviour was almost certainly driven by anxiety, I still found myself feeling irritated. At one point my mind wandered to a colleague I knew who tended to show off and how annoying I found this; I then recalled an old family friend who had done the same thing and how I had once heard my parents criticizing this trait. Reflecting later on my response, I recognized that this was a sensitive issue for me – probably because I struggle at times with how to share my successes appropriately. This alerted me to the importance of making sure I did not become provoked by Max's behaviour into showing my irritation.

Having become aware of this aspect of my own counter-transference enabled me to consider Max's behaviour calmly and objectively. I felt that it would be poorly regarded by at least some of his colleagues and would therefore have negative consequences in terms of his working relationships. For this reason, I decided to explore this issue later in the coaching process when Max would be feeling less anxious.

The importance of the coach's self-awareness in this context is clear. Only by knowing my own tendencies and psychology could I stop and recognize what I was bringing to the counter-transference. Having identified this, I was then able to separate it from my understanding of the client's dynamics.

I hope this chapter has conveyed the way in which my coaching practice is influenced by psychodynamic concepts which help me develop working hypotheses about the client based on observation and experience. In the next chapter, I explain how this approach guides my coaching interventions.

4 Getting alongside the client

When coaching, my aim is to enable clients to benefit their organizations and themselves by becoming better leaders and managers. This involves learning and change. This chapter examines the crucial issue of how to engage clients in this process. Although the coach may have an excellent understanding of an individual's dynamics and a clear picture of how they could do things more successfully at work, these insights will be worth little *unless the client is open to considering them.*

The psychodynamic model is particularly useful in explaining why highly intelligent clients willingly enter coaching to explore and improve their leadership abilities, only to resist doing just that. Through revealing the power of anxiety and the use of unconscious defence mechanisms, this perspective enables the coach to see through the surface of the client's narrative to the fears and feelings below. If we can address these with sensitivity and skill – if we can *get alongside our clients* – they will feel safe enough to take the risks involved in change and make use of new thoughts and ideas.

Holding in mind the client's need for psychological safety and tailoring my interventions accordingly is therefore a central strategy of my coaching practice. Both psychodynamic theory and neuroscience have underlined the central role of our emotions in determining how we respond to the outside world. They have highlighted the speed of our physiological response to perceived threats, however irrational, and the range of mechanisms we use in our attempts to restore a sense of security, calm and control. When a coach says something to a client without considering carefully enough how it will be experienced at an emotional level, they risk triggering a defensive reaction. Even though the point the coach made may be entirely reasonable and correct, and helpfully intended, if the client feels threatened, attacked, rejected, guilty or shamed, *it will not have been helpful.* Clients can respond to a premature, poorly phrased or overly blunt message in several ways. They may simply ignore it, change the subject, politely dismiss it, agree with it while hiding their true feelings, withdraw, become upset or respond with anger, even rage. Over the years I have experienced all these reactions to clumsy interventions of my own. Whatever the response, it is usually accompanied by a shutting down of the possibility of further exploration, at least for a time.

Of course we must challenge our clients' perceptions, thinking and behaviour if we are to help them develop. But this must be done in a way that feels safe. Head-on confrontation simply reinforces defences and threatens the coaching relationship – and therefore the whole process – as clients protect themselves from the painful thoughts and feelings that our comments have inadvertently triggered. This emphasis on the client's emotional experience of coaching shapes the strategies and techniques that follow.

Building the working alliance

The nature of the relationship that we establish with our clients is central to the coaching process. It forms the vehicle through which the coaching work takes place. It also forms part of the coaching process itself, as the client's gains are often closely linked to their experience of the relationship with the coach. Some clients find that the process of becoming close to and trusting the coach enough to make themselves vulnerable leads to a greater ability to allow other people close (see the case of Martine in Chapter 6). When coaching has been a positive experience for the client, the coach's presence and voice are internalized to become a permanent part of their inner world. We must also provide role models for the client through our ability to reflect, be empathic and honest, and manage our emotions and boundaries successfully.

However, to be fully effective, the coach–client relationship must go beyond the creation of mutual positive regard, trust and a good rapport. At its heart we must create a powerful *working alliance*. This describes the partnership between that part of the client that is *aligned with both the coach and the learning process* and that part of the coach that is *committed to both the client and the coaching task* (Horvath and Greenberg, 1994). This means that our ability to identify closely with a client must be balanced by our ability to remain in the role of coach with responsibility for addressing the client's work-related goals and tasks.

This can be a difficult balance to maintain. On the one hand our clients must feel that we are positioned alongside them and are *on their side*, while on the other we must retain enough objectivity to keep them focused on the process of change, despite the discomfort this may evoke. In this context, the coach also actively represents the interests of the client's organization and stakeholders. It is they who have invested in the coaching programme and who expect a return in the form of improved performance on the part of the client.

Without this working alliance, a friendly and trusting relationship may develop yet the coach and client may collude in a number of ways to avoid engaging fully in the real work that needs to be done. Alternatively, the work may proceed at a surface level but a lack of trust may inhibit the client from opening up and being honest. Even an excellent coach–client bond faces this risk during difficult or challenging moments in the work.

The coach–client relationship and the working alliance need to be developed as quickly as possible, starting at the first meeting, and sustained throughout the peaks and troughs of the coaching programme. Establishing and maintaining this deep and honest connection with the client is not an easy task. The first session with a client, which is often an exploratory meeting to decide whether the pair will work together, is a particularly critical point in the process. At this time, the client's anxieties and defences are likely to be strongest and the coach might also be at their most anxious. How the coach handles the situation will usually determine whether the coaching goes ahead.

This chapter outlines my strategies for building the coach–client relationship, developing a strong working alliance, recognizing the client's emotional and defensive patterns, and providing a sufficient sense of safety for them to open up to learning and change. I highlight those methods that are most critical at the outset of the coaching process – though they remain important throughout – and that are most directly influenced by the psychodynamic model. I use the case study of a client called Christina to illustrate some of these techniques.

The anxious new client

Christina

Christina was a senior executive in a large financial services company. Following her recent promotion, her boss and her HR director suggested coaching. When speaking to the latter on the telephone, it had been difficult to gain a sense of specific development needs or coaching objectives, although there had been a rather vague reference to managing stress. I was told that Christina readily agreed that coaching would be a good idea. It had taken some weeks, however, for the first meeting to take place as she had rescheduled the date several times.

Christina arrived for her first meeting with me about twenty minutes late. On arrival, she seemed flustered and irritable. She avoided eye contact and shook my hand with her fingertips. On the way to the coaching room, she told me how her taxi had been stuck in the traffic and how difficult it had been to get away from the office. She relaxed slightly when I acknowledged what a difficult journey she must have had and offered her refreshments but went on to complain about how inconvenient it was to come to my office and asked why the sessions could not take place at her office, as she had a demanding job and was extremely busy. Rather than engage directly with her question, I suggested that we come back to it towards the end of the session when she would have had a chance to see what coaching might be able to offer her.

Why did I choose to do this instead of explaining the advantages of having the coaching sessions at my office rather than hers? I hypothesized that behind Christina's complaints about the logistics and her lack of time lay a good deal of anxiety about exposing herself and her weaknesses to the scrutiny of a stranger. I felt she was expressing her anxiety both by distancing herself from me and by an indirect attack on me, her comments implying that she doubted I could offer her anything valuable enough to be worth her time. She may also have been trying – unconsciously – to hook me into an argument about where coaching took place as a way of avoiding the real work of the session. Under these circumstances, it was unlikely that a rational explanation from me about where I thought coaching worked best would influence her or be helpful.

Identifying anxiety

My interpretation of Christina's behaviour illustrates the importance I place on *recognizing, understanding and containing the anxiety that clients experience*, especially at the start of the coaching process. When I begin work with a client, I always hold in mind the likelihood that they will arrive at the meeting with at least some – and often a considerable degree of – anxiety about the coaching process, about me and about aspects of their work situation. Two of the most important insights that I have derived from the psychodynamic approach are that:

- Human beings become anxious much more easily than is generally realized.
- Anxiety manifests itself in a wide range of hidden and indirect ways.

If you take away nothing else from this book, it is worth remembering this. Understanding this enables me to realize that *negative or resistant behaviour may be anxiety-driven even if this does not appear to be obviously the case*. It is particularly important to hold anxiety in mind when the prospective client meets the coach for the first time. Anxiety will appear in many different guises. Sometimes, like Christina, the client has already postponed the session several times without obvious reason. Sometimes the client arrives late, on occasion having got inexplicably lost en route to the session. Other signs may include poor eye contact and other avoidant body language, being excessively apologetic, self-deprecating or self-critical, talking non-stop, showing off, self-justification through blaming or complaining about others, indirect attacks on the coach's competence or subtle rejection of the need for coaching at all.

In Christina's case, it seemed that she was dealing with her anxiety by avoiding engagement and expressing lively annoyance – with the taxi, with having to come to my office, with her workload and her colleagues – rather than by acknowledging any distress or vulnerability. This hypothesis enabled me to resist being distracted, undermined or provoked by her challenging behaviour. It prompted me instead to make a particular effort to get alongside Christina and increase her sense of psychological safety.

Expecting ambivalence

Closely connected to the anxiety that most clients feel when meeting the coach for the first time is a degree of *ambivalence* about the whole coaching process. I find it helpful to hold this in mind as well when decoding what might lie behind the fearful, distancing or negative behaviours that a client may often demonstrate at the first meeting. In Christina's case, her ambivalence, as well as her anxiety, was expressed through her repeated cancellations, her lateness and her complaints about having to come to my office.

Why are anxiety and ambivalence so common at the outset of the coaching process? First, coaching represents change. Any form of change, including change that the individual welcomes, evokes some difficult emotions. We experience uncertainty, the threat of loss in giving up familiar ways of doing things. We also risk failure. Any process that involves reflection, learning and development presents us with a challenge. Executive coaching is no exception. It brings us into contact, consciously or unconsciously, with the things we may not know or may not be good at; it may expose us as shamefully inadequate or reveal our vulnerabilities.

Most of our clients are successful professionals, yet this can heighten their ambivalence. They may think that their present way of doing things has delivered success, so why tamper with it? In addition, their apparent self-confidence may cover significant insecurity and lack of self-esteem. For these reasons, I assume that there will always be some mixed feelings on the client's part to the idea of coaching – between the wish to embrace it and the wish to turn back. Of course this varies between individuals, and will be less marked when coaching feels like a badge of honour rather than a badge of shame, but in my experience it is always present to some degree.

Some of the anxiety and ambivalence that clients bring to coaching will inevitably centre on the coach, especially at the beginning of the relationship. Many clients will perceive the coach, consciously or unconsciously, as a potentially critical authority figure. They may fear that the coach will scrutinize and assess them and pass judgement on their professional and personal worth. This can be intensified by the knowledge that the coach also has a relationship with senior stakeholders within the client's organization who have commissioned and funded the process. Knowing at a cognitive level that the coach is there to help and that a promise of confidentiality is in place around what is shared in the coaching room will not usually be enough on its own to assuage the client's feelings of vulnerability.

Offering structure

When faced with clear signs of anxiety and ambivalence from the client, my priority is to help them feel less anxious, as anxiety blocks their ability to relate to me, engage in the coaching process, reflect and learn. However, as the case of Christina shows, *I do not refer directly to their anxiety*. This would risk provoking a denial or a sense of being patronized and probably make it worse. Instead, *I behave in a way that is designed to reduce it*. Over time, I hope to help the client become more consciously aware of their own anxiety and manage it more effectively, but not at this early stage.

> In Christina's case, I felt that she would calm down more quickly if I provided some structure for our discussion. Therefore, having avoided engaging with the issue of where the sessions should take place, I asked her to use the flipchart to draw a simple diagram illustrating her role and responsibilities and those of her boss, peers, team and other key colleagues. This did seem to have a grounding effect. I then asked her to tell me about what she saw as the pressures of her role and her priorities for her part of the business.

Demonstrating empathy

> As Christina described her work situation, it soon became clear that she was struggling with a huge workload in the new, expanded role to which she had been recently promoted. She was also having difficulty in engaging some of her peer colleagues on a high-profile cross-functional project that she had been asked to lead by her CEO, in addition to her other responsibilities.
> Having listened to Christina for ten minutes or so, I became aware of an increasing sense of discomfort in myself. I noted the tension I was holding in my jaw, neck and shoulders and how shallow my breathing had become while listening to her speak. I waited for her to pause and then responded as follows: 'Listening to you, I am not surprised that you are concerned

about how you spend every minute of your time. Your description of your current workload has given me an almost physical sense of how stretched and overburdened you are. You clearly have a great deal of resilience.' Christina responded with a sigh, sat back in her chair and seemed to relax. I took a deep breath and relaxed too. It seemed that my acknowledgement of the reality of her workload – I had deliberately used the phrase 'how stretched and overburdened you are' rather than 'how stretched and overburdened you feel' – and the brief but emphatic positive feedback had been helpful.

Why had I chosen to make this intervention at this point instead of moving straight to exploring how Christina might deal more effectively with her situation? Expressing empathy in the right way and at the right time is crucial for getting alongside the client. It plays a central role in reducing their anxiety and ambivalence and begins to build a powerful rapport. Most new clients fear, consciously or unconsciously, that the coach will not be able truly to understand how the world looks and feels from their perspective. Therefore, from the outset, I listen carefully to the client's description of their internal and external reality and *empathize with their subjective experience*. Feeling and then expressing empathy does *not* mean that I necessarily share the client's views and perceptions or that I condone their behaviour. It does mean that I allow myself *to identify fully with them* in that moment and to experience as well as understand their thoughts and feelings. Skilfully conveyed, this not only reduces anxiety – as the client feels understood and accepted – but also creates a powerful connection and nourishes the embryonic working alliance. For Christina to calm down and begin to trust me, it was crucial that I demonstrated my understanding of how she was feeling. My empathy with her current experience of overload was a key moment in the session. It soothed her and helped her to engage.

Providing affirmation

Alongside empathy, affirmation is vital in helping a client feel recognized and appreciated. It played a small but significant part in my comments to Christina. The psychodynamic model explains that a level of *healthy narcissism* is part of the normal development of the ego. This represents the need for approval and affirmation that we look for from the significant people in our lives. The coach's affirmation is particularly important given the vulnerability that the coaching situation can evoke and the significance that the coach has as a potential authority figure. Our clients benefit from knowing that not only do we accept them as they are but that we recognize and admire their best qualities.

Gushing praise, trite compliments or patronizing accolades will of course backfire. However, when we find the right words at the right moment to affirm the client, this can be immensely helpful. These interventions consolidate the working alliance, boost the client's self-esteem and help them mobilize the courage they will need to take the risks that the coaching process represents.

Containing anxiety

Having helped Christina to relax and lower her defences a little through empathy and affirmation, I had to decide whether to draw her out further, and ask her what she wanted from coaching, or whether to offer my own thoughts on her current work situation. In considering this, I reflected to myself that Christina's working life seemed uncontained. It appeared that she rushed from one meeting to another, often arriving late, as she had today. She was going in to her office at 7am to get a head start on her seemingly never-ending task list and was working late into the night at home catching up on emails. Apart from concern about her work–life balance and her health, I felt that in her headlong rush to get as much done as quickly as possible, she was taking little time to reflect on her priorities, delegate effectively or invest in her work relationships. I felt that her demeanour and behaviour in our coaching session communicated both her anxiety and ambivalence about coaching *and* the extent to which she felt 'all over the place' at work, with no firm boundaries.

In deciding how to proceed, I also considered my early impressions of Christina's character and interpersonal style. On the basis of my briefing from HR, and from the short time we had spent together, she struck me as a task-focused, pragmatic individual with a quick mind and a tendency to impatience. She had shown the capacity to be influenced by my comments and I decided that I would be direct with her. I said that her workload seemed pretty uncontrollable at the moment – the endless list of tasks was driving her, rather than vice versa. Using a metaphor, I described her as clinging on with great determination to the neck of a bolting horse, doing all she could not to fall off, with no time to think about how to get back in the saddle, regain control and slow down.

In a further piece of affirmation, I observed that Christina's ability to deliver across a vast number of operational tasks was clearly excellent and had led to promotion. However, her new role was more strategic and in my view a different approach was called for. I emphasized the need for her to step back and identify her priorities; other tasks would have to be delegated, tackled less thoroughly, put on the back burner or dropped. This was the only way in which she would be able to make a really effective leadership contribution at the level that her CEO expected, spend time building relationships with key colleagues and get back in control of her work and her life.

With this intervention, I moved beyond empathy and affirmation, which were designed to reduce Christina's anxiety, to a more strategic approach. By my choice of words and style, I was attempting to *contain* her anxiety. The concept of *containment* comes from work on the psychological needs of the human infant (Bion, 1962; Winnicott, 1964). Containment is provided by a mother, or other carer, who is able to soothe the baby by identifying with and attending to its distress while remaining calm and not being overwhelmed by anxiety herself. It is a term used mainly by psychotherapists but it is relevant to any situation in which someone attempts to help others cope with anxiety or agitation and regain a sense of psychological safety. This concept is central to the Diamond Model that I developed during the recession of 2008 which outlines what leaders can do to help their staff feel as contained as possible during difficult and turbulent times (Sandler, 2009b).

Coaches can help to contain the client's anxiety in a number of ways. There is no simple formula; the coach must allow their intuition to guide what will feel containing to that particular individual. So what influenced me to intervene as I did with Christina?

With Christina, I moved in this direction as a result of my strong impression – physical as well as emotional and cognitive – that she was struggling to hold herself together in the face of multiple pressures and demands. I felt that she was feeling scattered and overwhelmed, emotionally as well as logistically. Although she had calmed down and relaxed a little, my priority remained to help provide a sense of psychological safety.

At this point, it felt right to take an active role as the seasoned guide who could offer clarity, structure and direction. Why? Partly in recognition of her own action-oriented style and partly because it would reassure Christina that *I* was not also feeling overwhelmed by her words or emotions. By describing her current desperate attempts to cope with her workload and pointing out the need for her to set limits and take a more strategic approach, I was also providing her with a reality check and this proved emotionally containing. Her relief came from hearing what she already knew was true but had been defending against by working even longer hours. She also felt encouraged by hearing her difficulties reframed in a way that made sense and held out the hope that she could do something about them. Finally, Christina responded positively to my direct style. It conveyed a sense of confidence and competence and reassured her that I would bring a practical, time-efficient approach to addressing her issues.

Christina's response to my description of the bolting horse and my recommended change of approach was a mixture of shock and relief. She acknowledged the accuracy of what I had said. She agreed that she wanted desperately to get back in control but could not see how. She asked whether I would be able to help her to achieve the goals I had described. I replied that I was confident that she could achieve them if she was willing to invest the time and effort needed, both inside and outside our sessions. I added that I would enjoy coaching her, as I liked the determination and intensity she brought to her work and the honesty and openness she had shown in our session. She asked me when we could start work.

Just before the end of the session, I briefly explained the benefits of clients leaving their offices and coming to a dedicated coaching space where they could think and reflect more productively. I pointed out that especially for people as busy as she, the journey to and from the session served as a time to prepare for and digest the work. She agreed immediately and it became clear that this was no longer an issue.

The need to contain anxiety can arise at any stage in the coaching process, even when a good working alliance has been established, the client is fully engaged and the work is going well. It is most likely to be needed with clients who regularly find it difficult to manage their own anxiety under certain kinds of pressure.

Kiran

A coaching client who illustrated this need well was Kiran, an executive in a global retail group. On one occasion, he arrived for his session in an agitated state, telling me that he had just learnt that his boss was leaving their company and that he was sure that this would lead to a restructure of his department and redundancies, including possibly his own. When he paused for breath, I commented – with feeling – that he must be shocked and disappointed at his boss's decision, which had seemingly come out of the blue, and also disconcerted by the uncertainty that this had created. I was using empathy as the first stage of helping Kiran contain his anxiety. I then moved to provide structure and a reality check.

Aware of both Kiran's value to his company and his tendency to underestimate his own worth, I calmly but firmly suggested that we take a step back and review the facts around his likely future, mentioning how difficult it can be to take a balanced view when one is upset. I helped him to recall his track record of achievement, his excellent appraisals and the positive feedback he had recently received from the managing director of the division. I also reminded him of his critical inner voice and its habit of becoming particularly strong when he felt out of control or unsure about the future. These interventions had the effect of reducing Kiran's anxiety, moderating his negative assumptions and helping him think more clearly and realistically about what had happened.

Kiran had been contained by the combination of concern and understanding I had shown for his distress on the one hand, and my calm and objective approach to assessing the facts on the other. This had soothed him emotionally and physiologically and helped restore his capacity to reflect.

Holding boundaries in mind

Part of providing a containing presence for our clients involves the capacity to *hold boundaries*. This term is often used in both the psychotherapeutic and coaching fields and is a helpful way of holding in mind at a symbolic level some of the important dividing lines that we must manage as part of the coaching process. It is frequently applied to confidentiality – the metaphorical line around the content of the one-to-one client–coach conversations that should not be crossed. It can also be used to refer to the start and finish times of the coaching sessions and the physical integrity of the coaching setting. Boundaries can also be considered in terms of roles, tasks and relationships.

Providing a containing presence for clients, for example, depends on the coach's capacity to stay within the boundaries of the working alliance, and to demonstrate both empathy and calm objectivity. The role of the client's line-manager and HR partner can also be considered in terms of boundaries; for example, we would say that a HR manager who asks to see the results of a confidential 360-degree feedback survey is crossing a boundary that should be respected.

The concept of boundaries can be particularly helpful in the early stages of coaching when many clients unconsciously test boundaries, often out of anxiety and sometimes because this is a characteristic part of their psychological and behavioural pattern.

Regina

For example, Regina, a prospective new client, cancelled her initial meeting with one of my supervisees on three consecutive occasions at short notice and with little explanation or apology. The coach's working hypothesis was that she might be feeling ambivalent about the idea of coaching, which had been suggested by her boss. He also wondered whether the client was unconsciously testing to see how serious he was about wanting to see her or how much he would put up with before drawing a line. When they finally met, it emerged that Regina was an individual who tended to push boundaries in all areas of her life, including at work, and this dynamic lay at the heart of her coaching issues.

The point here is that holding the notion of boundaries in mind helped the coach in a number of ways. He was able to think helpfully about possible messages that the client's behaviour was unconsciously conveying, to manage his counter-transference feelings that naturally included some irritation, and to make some rapid connections between how she had behaved towards him and the pattern of behaviour she showed towards others. He was able to establish an effective working relationship with this individual on the basis of noting – and in due course addressing – her challenging behaviour, without being either dominated or provoked by it. Without this early thinking about boundaries, there would have been less chance of a successful working alliance being created.

Using the client's transference

The case of Christina illustrates the ways in which anxiety and ambivalence can shape the behaviour of the client towards the coach, particularly at the outset of the coaching process. The psychodynamic model suggests that the way the client relates to the coach will also reflect the unconscious transference of aspects of important relationships earlier in their lives to this new relationship.

Transference can be most clearly seen at the start of the coaching process, when the client knows little about the coach or how they will behave; it will colour their attitude and approach, including how they express anxiety. At this point, clients often project onto the coach some of the attributes they expect, hope or fear they will find, based on their experience of other significant authority figures. In particular, those clients whose formative relationships have been painful, difficult or unfulfilling may expect negative behaviour or intent from the coach and behave accordingly. Some clients find closeness threatening and the intimacy of the coaching relationship difficult to tolerate. Others who take a suspicious or competitive stance in new relationships will re-enact these with the coach. Similarly, clients whose defence mechanisms involve idealizing others may idealize the coach; others may try to charm the coach or evoke their admiration.

Sometimes these transference dynamics are modified when the coach behaves in ways that do not fit the client's conscious or unconscious expectations; in other cases, clients will continue to transfer these perceptions, and act accordingly, throughout the coaching process. In any case, throughout the coaching process I regard the client's attitudes and behaviour towards me as a source of invaluable information about their inner landscape and their characteristic patterns of relating to others, including their work colleagues.

Maureen
Maureen was a good example of a client whose positive transference to me was helpful in understanding her dynamics. What I quickly noticed when we started work was that her attitude was really *too positive* to be based on experience or a realistic judgement of me and my work. Whatever I said was

listened to respectfully and from the outset she expressed her delight and good fortune at having me for her coach. The risk at this point was that Maureen and I had apparently got alongside each other so well that I might have colluded with her transference and accepted her positive feedback at face value.

Instead, I used Maureen's response to look for similar patterns in her other working relationships. Sure enough, it emerged that Maureen, a manager in a children's charity, tended to defend herself against anxiety, disappointment and fear of abandonment by taking a relentlessly positive view of her senior colleagues and other important figures in her life. Linked to this *idealization* was a tendency to *split* people into the wholly good and the wholly bad. She *demonized* some of the colleagues at her level in the organization, criticizing them for lack of commitment, laziness and shoddy work. These were people with whom she may well have been unconsciously competitive and was probably transferring to them feelings about her real-life siblings from whom she was estranged. Both Maureen's admiration and her condemnation had an extreme, polarized feel about them. The work of the coaching centred on helping her ease this defence and move slowly towards a more realistic way of relating to her colleagues at all levels, and to me.

Therefore, I believe the transference should be regarded as an unavoidable and natural part of the client's response to the coach – and a helpful source of insight – rather than something to be feared or avoided. Transference does *not* automatically mean that the client will become excessively dependent on us. Nor is it something unwanted that we should try to discourage as some coaches seem to believe. Transference simply *occurs* and should be used as both an illuminating route to understanding our clients and a guide as to how best to work with them.

What not to do

This chapter has described some of my strategies for getting alongside my clients and building the working alliance. It may be helpful to illustrate one of the many ways in which coaches may inadvertently upset, anger or shame their clients. A particularly explosive reaction can be provoked when a coach fails to apply a sufficiently thoughtful filter between their theories about the client's inner world and their interventions in the coaching session.

In Chapter 3, I suggested that coaches should develop working hypotheses to explain their clients' behaviour based on careful listening and observation, and then seek further evidence to confirm, modify or contradict these views. What I would like to underline here in the strongest possible terms is that even when we feel confident that our understanding is accurate, *this does not mean that we should necessarily communicate our insights directly to the client.* This statement may seem obvious. Yet I emphasize it because long experience as a coaching supervisor has taught me that this is a common mistake. Often it stems from the coach's urge to move as quickly as possible from *understanding* something about their client to *doing* something with it in the form of an active intervention. This is understandable and may reflect a commendable focus on results. However, when unchecked, this enthusiasm can lead to inappropriate timing and insufficient care over what is said, which triggers the defensive responses that are best avoided. For this reason, I repeatedly remind my supervisees that the role of working hypotheses is to guide the understanding of the coach and influence what they do and say. They are not to be explicitly expressed to the client. Coaches must develop the capacity to contain the urge to share their thinking wholesale and instead find the right time and the right words for a skilful intervention.

For some coaches, the tendency to communicate their thoughts too transparently may arise from a sense of discomfort with the idea of holding strong views about their clients of which the clients remain unaware. They feel that this is somehow too judgemental and goes against the principle of mutual respect and honesty that should characterize the coaching conversations. Here, my perspective is different. I believe that the skilful, experienced coach will inevitably perceive and understand things about their clients that the clients themselves do not see and would probably disagree with if they were explicitly articulated. It is these perceptions and this understanding that will allow the coach, over time, to help clients make constructive changes and meet their goals. But this can only happen if the coach is confident in taking responsibility for bringing their expertise to the process and is able to accept that their role involves an element of leadership as well as partnership.

Denise

A good example of this arose recently when I was supervising a colleague who was describing his third session with a client called Denise, a manager in an engineering firm. In this session, she had spoken with a great deal of feeling about her difficult relationship with her boss whom she described as domineering and having a low opinion of her. From a brief discussion about her family background in the first coaching session, the coach knew that Denise had a difficult relationship with her father, from whom she was estranged. He formed the plausible working hypothesis that the client may have been projecting onto her boss some of the attributes and behaviour that she had experienced in her father. He felt that if this was so, there was a risk that she would react in a similar way – by withdrawing and feeling angry and hurt – rather than by engaging more constructively in building a better relationship with her boss. However, when the coach described what he had said to the client, it was clear that this intervention had not been a success. His exact words had been, 'I think unconsciously you're transferring your feelings about your father onto your boss.'

Predictably, the client did not react well to this statement. She was not a naturally psychologically minded individual and had shown her anxiety at the outset of coaching around what the process would involve, emphasizing her preference for a practical, action-based approach. The coach's statement, though in all probability correct, was phrased much too baldly. Denise reacted defensively, feeling humiliated and criticized. In all probability it had activated her critical inner voice, which was saying, 'What kind of idiot confuses their boss with their father?' At the same time, she may have been asking herself, 'Who does he think he is, trying this Freudian rubbish on me!' At an unconscious level, the coach's remarks may also have been experienced as quite threatening, as the idea that her boss might be like her father made her anxious. Consciously she simply felt negative about him and cancelled the following session.

While another client might have been open to the coach making an explicit link between father and boss – though in a more tentative and tactful way – this particular client needed a more roundabout approach. The coach might have said something like, 'I get the sense that your boss's behaviour has been really upsetting for you – it sounds as if you feel both hurt and angry with him?' If this comment-cum-question had hit the mark and the client had agreed and felt understood, he would have strengthened the coaching relationship. He would have helped her become more in touch with her emotions and opened up space for her to reflect on why her boss had aroused such a strong reaction.

If the coach felt that it was important for Denise to be aware of the link with her father in order to work effectively on her relationship with her boss, he could have pointed out that we all bring with us to our work relationships some of the experiences we have had in significant relationships elsewhere in our lives. This might have opened the door to asking her – rather than telling her – about a possible link with her father.

Managing the counter-transference

I shall end this chapter with some thoughts on managing the counter-transference. While clients transfer to us some of the patterns laid down elsewhere, as coaches we bring our own emotional and psychological patterns and history to our relationships with clients. It is natural that we should have a multi-layered response to each client – to their appearance, voice, attitude, style and behaviour, as well as what we have been told about them before the first meeting – and this will partly reflect our own inner landscape.

The idea that it is possible or desirable to have no strong reactions to, or to make no judgements about, our clients is misplaced. Like the transference, the counter-transference simply exists. However, it is very important that we are able to recognize and manage our thoughts and feelings in relation to the client – to separate what is to do with them and what is to do with us. This enables us to remain in role and fully engage in the working alliance. Most critically, we must understand the difference between using our counter-transference as a rich source of data about our clients – sometimes a tremendously helpful way of understanding them – and unconsciously allowing it to drive or nudge us into an inappropriate stance.

It is at the first meeting with a new client that our counter-transference responses to the client may be clearest. It is also the time when we are likely to be most anxious. We do not know exactly what to expect and even the most confident coach is likely to be asking themselves some questions. Will this person want to work with me? If not, why not? What effect would that have on my ongoing relationship with the client's organization? Will I feel able to help them? Will I want to work with them? The challenge here is to acknowledge and manage – not to suppress – this anxiety and to have the self-awareness to anticipate how it might manifest itself.

There are several other common problems that can arise when we do not manage our counter-transference well. One consists of over-identifying with the client and taking on too much of their anxiety, anger or other emotions. This can lead to collusion with the client's blind spots and the loss of the essential element of objectivity that helps them confront reality and achieve constructive change (see the case of Paul in Chapter 6).

Another pitfall is *working harder than the client* to make the coaching a success. This is a sure sign that we are taking on too much responsibility for the process. We need to refocus, explore the client's real feelings about the coaching and, if the work continues, ensure that *they* take responsibility for their own engagement and progress.

A third difficulty occurs when coaches find themselves losing confidence and feeling criticized or attacked by a client when there is no real evidence that this is the case.

Alexandra

This was a dynamic that Alexandra, one of my supervisees, fell prey to when she was coaching an investment banker. A self-contained, undemonstrative individual, this client had been sent for coaching to prepare him for promotion to the executive committee of the division in which he worked. He was brilliant in his highly mathematical area of technical expertise and had several degrees, including a PhD from Yale. The coach reported finding him critical and was convinced that he did not feel she could offer him anything helpful. When we explored this case in supervision, it was clear that she was feeling anxious and had lost her usual confidence in her coaching ability, though she could provide no clear sign that the client was in fact critical of her.

We explored the possibility that the client was using the defence of *projective identification* and was unconsciously exporting and mobilizing in her his own anxiety or lack of confidence. However, there was little evidence for this hypothesis. We then considered instead what this particular client might have triggered in the coach. It emerged that, due to some difficulties in her adolescence, the coach had failed her A-levels and not gone to university. Although she had succeeded in earning a degree from the Open University later in life, and had done well professionally, this had left her with some insecurity about her academic track record. It appeared that this highly qualified and intelligent client had unwittingly brought this insecurity back to life. On reflection, the coach concluded that she had been *projecting* onto the client her own self-critical feelings and then feeling attacked or rejected by him. Once in conscious awareness, this problem resolved itself and the coaching proceeded well.

A final example of unhelpful counter-transference is when we find ourselves becoming excessively critical, impatient or angry with a client, which can damage both the coaching relationship and the work.

Sandra

This happened when I started coaching a client called Sandra to whom I found myself having quite a negative reaction. Sandra came to see me for coaching at the suggestion of her boss. A senior clinician in the National Health Service, she wanted support in dealing with stress and overload. She also felt that she had been passed over for promotion and wanted to ensure that this did not happen again. When I greeted Sandra, I was struck by her unprepossessing appearance. Her hair was scraped back in an elastic band, her blouse was ill-fitting and her shoes were dirty and scuffed. The impression she gave was one of self-neglect. This impression continued when Sandra told me about her situation at work. Her narrative seemed to consist of a catalogue of complaints and I found the word 'victim' flashing into my mind. I also had the sense that my role was simply to be a sympathetic and supportive audience.

The strength of my emotional response prompted me to reflect on it in my own mind during the session. True, this client was not proving easy to engage with but she was no worse than many others whose anxiety or ambivalence manifested itself in resistant behaviours at the first meeting. Why had she triggered my irritation to this degree? I reminded myself that my own inner landscape includes a fear of feeling powerless. My characteristic way of dealing with problems or anxieties is to be proactive – to *do* something about them. This client's passive aggressive style was putting me uncomfortably in touch with that fear and my immediate reaction had been to feel critical of her. Unconsciously, this had also helped me to reassure myself that her suffering was not really that bad – she could do something about it if she really wanted to. This insight enabled me to feel less negative and more open to listening and understanding Sandra's experience.

As the coaching process unfolded, it seemed clear to me that this client felt uncomfortable with her own anger and tended to deny it and project it onto others. She then experienced them as victimizing her and responded with a mixture of passive aggression and self-damaging behaviour. My counter-transference had contained important clues, therefore, to Sandra's internal world and typical patterns. But it was only by becoming aware of the element of my reaction that reflected my own patterns that I was able to stay both connected to the client and objective enough to help her address these important issues.

For these reasons, it is vital that coaches have a high level of self-awareness and the capacity to apply that awareness as we respond to the client during the course of the work. We must develop the ability to observe, not suppress, our counter-transference reactions. We must manage them skilfully rather than being controlled by them. In the here and now of a session this is not always possible. This is one of the most important reasons why high-quality, regular coaching supervision is so important. It provides the essential space in which we can reflect on and adjust as necessary our responses to the client. In this way, we can remain fully engaged in the working alliance with our clients – committed to their welfare, to the coaching task and to the interests of their organization. With all this in mind, we can get alongside them and take steps to reduce their anxiety, thus providing the psychological safety that they need to learn and change.

5   Developing insight
    and enabling change

Before I set out the psychodynamically-influenced strategies and techniques that I use, I shall describe a single session with a client called Zoe. This illustrates how I set out to work with clients *at two levels*. By engaging with their current material, I aim to address both their specific needs and the broader developmental issues of which they may or may not be aware. The session also highlights how insight can promote change. It shows the close link between developing this client's self-awareness, helping her to gain insight into others and enabling her to make constructive behavioural changes.

Zoe

Zoe was an executive within the fast-moving consumer goods sector who had recently moved from a specialist function to a general management role as head of a large production team. She had requested coaching as a way of helping her navigate this transition and extend her people management skills. Zoe began one of our coaching sessions by telling me about her disappointment and frustration with her new deputy, Marianne, whom she had recruited from another part of the company. One reason she had been so pleased to have Marianne join the team was that it would be her job to deal with a particularly difficult individual lower down the departmental hierarchy who was creating a toxic atmosphere in her area of work. The performance, attitude and behaviour of this longstanding employee had been causing problems for some time, as Zoe had discovered when she took on her new role. No previous manager had addressed the issue and Marianne had been recruited partly for her reputation for toughness with poor performers.

I listened carefully while Zoe recounted what had happened. Apparently, Marianne had taken an extremely direct approach to the poor performance issue – as Zoe had wanted – and the result was that the difficult individual was now threatening to bring a grievance against her. When the HR director had looked into what had happened, he found that Marianne had made errors in the way she handled a critical meeting. He told Zoe that, were the grievance brought, it could possibly be upheld.

Having empathized with how Zoe was feeling about this unfortunate situation, I explored in some detail what urgent steps she could take to limit the damage, avert the grievance and restore Marianne's authority. This was helpful and important but I was keen to move the focus in due course to Zoe's own contribution to the situation that she now found herself in.

In particular, I was concerned that Zoe seemed to have underestimated the support and oversight that Marianne needed to make a successful transition into a new department and a demanding new role. Zoe had seen Marianne as a solution – she would ease the heavy workload and deal with the pressing problem of the poor performer. This was partly because she had taken Marianne's extremely confident manner at face value and concluded that she would not need, or indeed want, any guidance from her new boss. I felt that Zoe had failed to see the natural anxiety and tension that probably lay below Marianne's outward persona as she moved into her new job, keen to succeed and particularly to show Zoe that she could deal with poor performers.

By helping Zoe slow down and analyse her own reactions and behaviour, she was able to learn from the experience at a number of levels. Specifically, she felt that she should have anticipated that Marianne would need help in dealing with a complex and longstanding performance situation and she concluded that she should have provided coaching and support to her around this issue.

The psychodynamic difference

I would like to step back for a moment and review my coaching practice in this session. Up to this point it could be described as flexible, practical and results-focused. I have explored my client's specific issue with her in some depth, enabled her to reassess her management of a new team member and helped her work out how to do this more effectively in the future. However, this description could apply to a number of different approaches to executive coaching. How does the psychodynamic approach make my practice different? To answer this question, let us return to the session with Zoe.

Although Zoe had decided that in future she would approach situations like that with Marianne differently, I was keen to dig deeper and understand *why* she had misread the situation. When I encouraged her to reflect further on what had happened, Zoe recalled that there had in fact been several indications that Marianne was not as sure of herself as she had seemed. Yet Zoe had ignored them in her wish to see her new deputy as competent and self-sufficient.

This realization enabled us to explore in some depth what had got in the way of Zoe acting on the signs that Marianne was struggling – signs that she had seen but had also not seen. I encouraged Zoe to focus on how she had been feeling over the last week or so. This led to a breakthrough moment when Zoe made the link between her failure to see how Marianne really was and her own anxiety about two difficult issues that were facing her area of the business. She had dealt with her anxiety by moving into action mode and focusing only on her list of tasks. She had treated Marianne in an uncharacteristically two-dimensional way, as a solution to a problem rather than as a new team member who needed attention and direction as she made the transition into the team. She had then become annoyed when Marianne did not perform as planned.

Zoe was thoughtful following these important insights into the domino effect of her own unacknowledged anxiety. She commented that 'if she did not learn to manage her feelings and behaviour more effectively when under pressure, the same situation could easily arise again'. I agreed and we spent some time considering what she could do. She decided to seek more support internally, both from her line-manager and a mentor and to clear some 'stop and think' time in her diary each week. She felt that these steps would help her from starting to feel too worried or overwhelmed by the challenges of her role.

Having understood what happened if her anxiety went unmanaged, Zoe experienced another level of learning when she made the further link between 'feeling worried' and 'feeling irritated'. She realized that for her, the one often expressed itself as the other – as had happened in relation to Marianne. She resolved to use a growing sense of irritation as an early warning sign to slow down, take stock and identify and address any underlying anxieties.

Zoe also decided not only to invest more time one-to-one with new colleagues, including internal hires, but to pay particular attention to subtle signs that they may be experiencing difficulties even if they insisted that everything was fine. She was determined to become more sensitive to what was going on below the surface and to focus on creating the conditions in which her team members felt able to share their concerns. To foster this approach, she decided to institute dedicated coaching sessions at which developmental issues would be addressed, rather than the usual list of business items.

Over the following months, Zoe demonstrated her growing ability to tune in to her own emotional state. She became more aware of what made her anxious and became better at acknowledging her anxiety so that she could avoid throwing herself into action instead of stopping to reflect. She talked difficult issues through with her mentor on a regular basis and when necessary asked for support from her boss. As well as becoming more aware of her own responses under pressure, Zoe became skilled at reading her colleagues' emotions and behaviour while remaining both empathic and objective. Zoe's self-awareness and these new behavioural strategies stemmed from the session described above, which revolved around the incident with Marianne, and made an important contribution to her developing leadership.

I hope that this material illustrates the difference that the psychodynamic approach can make. By drawing on psychodynamic concepts and techniques, I find I can work at greater depth and address the *invisible obstacles* that keep clients trapped in dysfunctional emotional and behavioural patterns, despite their best efforts to change. In Zoe's case, it was going *beyond* the awareness that she should have handled her colleague differently that made this session so important. It was unearthing the links between Zoe's unacknowledged anxiety, her excessive task focus, her blindness to her colleague's needs and her irritation that provided the most significant learning. Only by surfacing and challenging this unconscious defensive pattern could Zoe be confident of not making the same mistake the next time she was under pressure and felt anxious.

The psychodynamic approach also helps me to understand the importance of helping my clients not only to become more aware of the parts of themselves they have previously defended against, but also to become more *tolerant and accepting of what they experience as disappointing or shameful aspects of themselves*. It is when they learn to accept their less congenial qualities as a normal part of themselves – though without allowing them to govern their behaviour – that they are able to grow in confidence, become more able to attend to their own needs appropriately and more able to respond appropriately to the needs of others. In this way, over the course of each coaching programme, I continually foster a *subtle but significant shift in the client's relationship with themselves*.

Of course, clients vary in their ability to achieve these internal shifts. Some embrace the opportunity and transform their leadership capacities with astonishing speed. Others take worthwhile and often inspiring steps in this direction. While a few will remain virtually immune to the process, experience has shown me that the vast majority of executive coaching clients can benefit from an approach that understands and addresses their underlying psychological dynamics. Indeed, I believe that only this will give them the freedom to feel, think and do things differently at work in an authentic and sustainable way.

From a psychodynamic perspective, working at these tasks strengthens the client's *ego*. This is the mature, regulating, reality-based part of the self that is capable of balancing the individual's needs with those of other people, and of learning from experience. This work is also aimed at loosening the grip of the client's *superego*, the critical inner voice that drives guilt and shame and leads to self-blame and blaming of others.

As I highlighted in Chapter 4, the psychodynamic approach opens the door not only to a deeper understanding of my clients but also to an emphasis on *how* I communicate with them. It is important to reiterate here that holding the clients' need for psychological safety continually in mind remains central to my practice. Even when a good working alliance has been established and the client is fully engaged, I strive to avoid triggering defensive reactions. Choosing the best moment, the appropriate words and the right tone and body language to communicate is crucial. I focus continually on stretching the awareness of my clients – and motivating them to do things differently – while also protecting their sense of self.

This point is particularly important when coaching clients begin to recognize the unhelpful nature of some of their patterns. If we encourage them to modify longstanding ways of coping with difficult thoughts and feelings, we must also help contain the anxiety that this process will evoke. For instance, when the task-focused high-flyer whose anxiety has driven her into premature action develops insight into her behaviour, she experiences both a gain and a loss. On the positive side, she learns to become more reflective and measured in the way she handles her leadership role, with clear benefits to herself and her business. On the negative side, however, she must acknowledge the 'weakness' represented by her previous, dysfunctional behaviour. Similarly, when a relationship-focused manager who prides himself on being a kind and reasonable person becomes more aware of his hidden anger, he is able to manage it more appropriately but must also come to terms with having a 'bad' part of himself.

For these reasons, the coaching techniques that I share here are designed to ensure that in-depth work takes place carefully, responsibly and with the client's psychological wellbeing always in the forefront of the coach's mind.

My coaching practice

To illustrate more fully some of the psychodynamically informed coaching techniques that I find most helpful in developing clients' insight and promoting behavioural change, I shall draw on my work with Adam, the 45-year-old divisional managing director of a large IT services company.

Adam

Adam came for coaching at the suggestion of the Group HR director as he was responsible for leading the restructure of his division to make it more fit for purpose in a highly competitive marketplace. This was taking place in the context of a company-wide culture change driven by a new CEO. Adam was thought to be doing a reasonable job overall but was seen as needing to become more effective at managing poor performance and to develop a leadership style that was more passionate and inspiring.

At one of our earliest coaching sessions, Adam talked a great deal about the problems he was having with two of the members of his senior team whom he had inherited when he was promoted to MD six months earlier, one of which had unsuccessfully applied for Adam's job. He felt that they were resistant both to his leadership and to the new working practices and culture that the organizational restructure required. Repeated conversations with these individuals had resulted in little positive change. Adam's body language and tone of voice indicated how strongly he felt about this. As he emphasized the amount of time and energy this issue was taking up, his face flushed, he leaned forwards, twisted his hands and his voice rose in volume.

I responded with empathy, saying how frustrating this situation sounded and that I could understand his feeling quite angry about it. His immediate response was to sit up in his chair, shake his head vigorously and insist that he did not feel angry, simply a little concerned as it was taking up a lot of time. He added that no-one was to blame, it was just one of those things and he would have to sort it out. I felt that I had inadvertently triggered a defensive response despite the tentative and sympathetic tone in which I had made my comment. I reflected on the gap that seemed to exist between Adam's emotional experience and his conscious awareness. Given his defensive response, I decided to return to this theme rather than pursue it then and there.

Later in the session, Adam told me about his boss, the Group CEO, whom he found distant and unsupportive. Again, he showed non-verbal signs of anger but pre-empted me by saying that he was not angry about it, pointing out that at his level in the organization it was unreasonable to expect a hands-on line-manager and that he was, in any case, not really that bad. It was as if he was defending himself against the criticism that he was being too negative or angry.

I formed the impression that Adam became quite quickly angry and upset about difficult workplace relationships but seemed out of touch with or scared of his feelings and found them hard to acknowledge. He used the defences of *rationalization* and *denial* when his emotions threatened to bubble over or he anticipated criticism. I developed the hypothesis that he was experiencing an *inner conflict*, largely unconscious, between the part of him that was furious with his colleagues, and wanted to draw me in to criticizing them too, and the part of him that was fearful or ashamed at losing control or being angry.

Recognizing difficult emotions – the 'mixed feelings' technique

Coaching clients vary a great deal in their ability to identify and willingness to acknowledge their true thoughts and feelings. From the outset, I look for evidence of their level of awareness and openness and try to assess how easily the individual's defensive reactions are triggered and what form these reactions take. Some clients are extremely prickly and quick to reject almost any observation I might offer, in which case great care and patience is needed. Others are more open and less defensive and this can allow for a much faster pace of work. Irrespective of this, the key is always to find a way to make it sufficiently psychologically safe for the client to recognize thoughts and feelings that they are – consciously or unconsciously – unwilling to acknowledge.

In Adam's case, I could have tried to raise his awareness of being angry by sharing my observations of his non-verbal behaviour in the session. However, my view was that, however sensitively done, this would have felt shaming for him and would have led to embarrassment and denial. Instead, I used a technique that I hoped would avoid triggering his defences. It draws on the psychodynamic concept of inner conflict and I use it a good deal. I find that it is often successful in helping clients own previously denied thoughts and feelings. It involves suggesting that the client would naturally have *mixed feelings* about an issue or relationship and then describing each set of feelings in *sympathetic terms* to make it as easy as possible for them to identify with both sides. This also introduces the client to the idea that it is entirely normal to have conflicting views and emotions about all sorts of things and that it can be helpful to recognize and explore them.

When the chance arose to use this technique in my next session with Adam, I took it. This time he had been complaining further about his two direct reports and also about one of his Group head office colleagues whose error in a policy paper had involved him in hours of extra work. My comments went something like this:

> When I reflect on these difficult situations that you've been telling me about, I feel for you. It seems to me that on the one hand there is, totally understandably, a part of you that becomes really frustrated and fed up at having to deal with colleagues who aren't doing their bit. On the other hand, there is an important part of you that has high professional standards, is self-controlled and feels that you should always take a calm and rational approach to this kind of situation. Would you agree?

Adam responded positively to this intervention. He seemed to relax and became more thoughtful. He agreed with what I had said and for the first time acknowledged that he did find these problems 'annoying'. He said he felt 'quite cross' sometimes but would immediately set this feeling aside as he 'did not believe that anger ever solved anything'. His approach was just to 'get on and deal with things' as best he could.

Even this limited admission represented a significant step towards Adam becoming more reflective and self-aware and I was keen to see how I could take it further. The hypothesis guiding me in this direction was that fear of his own anger was stopping Adam from being as direct and authoritative as he needed to be with his under-performing team members. I also suspected that denying his negative feelings was responsible for the perceived lack of passion and impact in his leadership more generally.

Understanding irrational beliefs

The psychodynamic perspective has helped me to understand that irrational or magical beliefs can take root and linger beyond childhood even within sophisticated adults. This can sometimes mean that clients struggle to feel confident about the difference between thinking or feeling something and acting on it. I wondered if this applied to Adam.

When I gently asked **Adam** why he felt it so important to only allow himself 'sensible' thoughts and feelings, it became clear that it did. He replied, 'Of course I must remain sensible – it would be appalling for the MD to be unprofessional and start shouting and swearing, however annoying the situation!' His language revealed his fear and assumption that simply acknowledging his anger would lead inexorably to unacceptably aggressive behaviour towards his colleagues. I realized that as long as Adam fused thoughts and feelings with uncontrollable action in his mind, he would continue to censor himself and his ability to deal more effectively with his colleagues would continue to be compromised as a result.

Reframing the problem

Depending on a client's level of self-awareness and their capacity to reflect on my comments without reacting defensively, I find it can be helpful to play back my understanding of what is taking place and my perspective on what needs to change. This functions to reframe the client's problem in a way that can move their own perceptions and thinking forward. As indicated already, however, empathy and affirmation must accompany this approach if it is to work well.

I was keen to try and take Adam past the continuing suppression of his emotional energy. Having heard the latest news about the still recalcitrant team members, I said something like this:

It seems to me that one of your real strengths is your ability to behave in a calm and rational manner with your colleagues regardless of how you might be feeling about them or their behaviour. We all know managers who lose control and take a bull in a china shop approach and this can do a lot of damage. Your wish to be consistently self-controlled and professional in your dealings with others does you great credit.

That said, while I would completely agree that you should remain calm and professional when discussing performance problems with your team members, I think that your concern not to show any sign of anger or frustration at all may be resulting in a low-key delivery and a low impact message. You have spoken to each of them several times but they just don't seem to be hearing you. My feeling is that you could allow some of your passion for doing the right thing for the company to show in the way you speak to them, you would be able to convey much more clearly how seriously you regard the situation. This does *not* mean losing your temper. But it would mean allowing a little more emotion to show. I think that this would significantly increase your impact and effectiveness without compromising your commitment to professionalism. What do you think?

By this stage in the coaching process, Adam had become considerably more self-aware and, having reflected on what I had said, he agreed that it made sense. However, this did not mean that he was ready and willing to try and modify his behaviour in the way I outlined.

This situation is not unusual in coaching – the client has arrived at the point, through your efforts and their own, of understanding what they need to do differently to be more effective. Yet some remain hesitant or anxious about trying something new, while others attempt implementation but struggle to carry through their changed behaviour.

Visualizing the two ends of the spectrum

There is no single technique guaranteed to help clients move from insight to action. Often it is a matter of patiently continuing work – exploring what is hindering them, planning and practising new strategies, and encouraging them to experiment and take one small step at a time. Frequently, I have found that a client is held back by the fear that even a small step in the new direction might result in a kind of unstoppable slide to the other end of the behavioural scale.

I suspected that Adam, with his magical belief that thought and feeling equalled action, might be struggling with just this anxiety. It turned out that he was. On the one hand, he made it clear that he agreed with my description and wanted to bring more emotion to his leadership and management style. On the other hand, he was extremely concerned about turning into the kind of ranting, intimidating boss he despised and was afraid that any change would lead to a slippery slope.

Why does this fear have such a tight grip on some clients? After all, at a rational level, the concept of making a small rather than a large change seems straightforward. The psychodynamic model is extremely helpful here. When a client like Adam expresses *such* horror at the idea of behaving in a particular way, this can indicate a powerful – but unconscious – part of him that would like to behave in just this way. He has unconsciously defended against this unacceptable part by denying his emotions and taking an overly rationalized approach to difficult interpersonal situations. Being encouraged to step even a little closer towards it can trigger anxiety and resistance.

> Yet in Adam's case, the price he paid for this inhibition was three-fold: first, I had experienced how his anger and frustration leaked out unhelpfully in non-verbal ways; second, he was often left exhausted by the effort of denying and controlling his feelings; and third, as we have seen, this dynamic resulted in an ineffective, low-impact communication style with poor results.

In this kind of situation, I do *not* share this hypothesis with the client. It would in nearly every case be met with indignant denial and would do more harm than good. Instead, I acknowledge the client's fear of being catapulted, as a result of one small step, to the other end of the behavioural spectrum and I empathize with their need to feel confident that changing their style will be a safe and managed process. I then usually use a simple but powerful visual technique that I have found has a containing effect and helps to reduce the client's anxiety. I draw a long horizontal line on the whiteboard and label each end with extreme, opposite versions of the behaviour under discussion.

> When I used this with Adam, I wrote 'Extremely controlled and unemotional' at one end of the line and 'Extremely angry and emotional' at the other and marked the mid-point between them. I then drew a face at each end with an expression that reflected the respective approaches. I asked Adam to indicate where on this spectrum he thought his current style fell. When he pointed to within 10 per cent of the 'Extremely controlled and unemotional' end, I agreed that this seemed about right and put a cross on the line to mark the position. I asked him how far he would consider moving from that point and he replied that he would want to stay on the 'controlled' side of the mid-point. I suggested that if he moved only 15 to 20 per cent towards the centre, this would be ample. I marked where on the line this would place him. I explained that, in my opinion, this shift would bring him close enough to an area of middle ground in which a more effective, balanced approach could be taken.

Experience has proved that this technique can be helpful in calming and containing the client's anxiety in the face of desired but frightening behavioural change. Its visual nature activates the right side of the brain and it helps to provide a reassuring and concrete representation of the fact that a small shift and a large shift are not the same thing. The picture of the spectrum, the boundary between the two sides and the cross indicating their new position – still on the same side as before, just a little nearer the centre – can be easily and reassuringly brought to mind by the client. As always, it will work best when the client knows that their fear of the slippery slope or 'catapult effect' has been heard and fully understood by the coach.

> Visualizing the behavioural spectrum worked well with Adam for whom it was the catalyst he needed to try out a different style of conversation with his team members. I supported his careful preparation and when the conversations went well, he was immensely encouraged. Further planning and preparation led to further success. A modest increase in his emotional range led to noticeably greater authority, confidence and impact in his leadership style. He – and his boss – were delighted with the results.

Tolerating difficult emotions – the 'normalizing' technique

As well as helping clients to become more aware of their emotions, I aim to increase their capacity to become *more tolerant* of those thoughts and feelings that they perceive as irrational, unreasonable or silly. These are often defended against and, even when the client recognizes them, they may well be hidden from the coach. A technique for reducing the client's discomfort is to *anticipate* what they might be feeling embarrassed about and then make a comment that *normalizes* these feelings. I also try to put these feelings in a wider context to indicate how common they are.

Clive

For example, when coaching Clive, a highly qualified researcher working in a government department, we focused on the issue of his low self-confidence in relation to his career prospects. Despite a stellar track record and evidence that he was considered by his senior colleagues to be a rising star in his department, he was plagued by the fear that he would not be promoted or possibly not even retained after his current five-year contract ended. He also felt sure that his peers were producing better quality work than he was. At the same time, he berated himself for being silly, saying that another part of him knew that this was not really the case.

Although Clive had a reasonable level of self-awareness about this issue and knew that his fears were largely irrational, this did not stop him worrying. I decided to try to *normalize* his career anxieties to help him to become less preoccupied by them. So on the next occasion when he raised this issue, I wondered aloud whether his fears partly stemmed from a secret feeling that he was actually a bit of a fraud who had somehow managed to fool people into thinking that he was a great deal cleverer than he really was. Perhaps he had done so well through some freakish stroke of good luck and now lived in fear that one day his colleagues would see through him.

As soon as I said this, Clive laughed with relief, saying: 'That's exactly it! I *do* feel a fraud and don't really deserve to be here but then I feel stupid for thinking that.' I asked him if he knew that this feeling was a common phenomenon among highly successful people. He looked surprised and said 'no', so I explained that individuals who were especially gifted in a particular area were often susceptible to feeling insecure, as it felt as if their success came to them too easily. I gave an example of another client I had worked with, an award-winning scientist, who had expressed exactly the same feeling of being a fraud; he had worried that the outside world saw him as being much better-read and better-informed than was really the case and lived in fear of the 'killer question' that would one day expose his ignorance.

Clive found this intervention helpful. It helped him to become less ashamed of his 'silly' worries, as well as reducing his anxiety. This increased his confidence and freed up emotional energy to focus on becoming more effective in other areas of his working life.

This technique involves articulating what I suspect are the client's secret fears in a way that makes them sound entirely normal and commonplace. I often reinforce this by telling the story of an impressive individual who had the same thoughts and feelings. It is important that I also *model* a tolerant and accepting attitude towards them through the matter-of-fact and sympathetic way in which I deliver my message. The coach's behaviour as well as words influences the client. I was careful not to tell Clive what he was thinking. I did not say 'You feel a fraud'. Instead, I wondered aloud whether perhaps his fears might stem partly from this feeling. This oblique approach makes it much easier for the client to consider the point. If it is offered as a possible insight that the client can accept or reject, they are far less likely to react defensively.

Focusing on the 'hot spot'

One of the challenges we face as coaches is the client who arrives at a session with plenty of material to share and several possible themes to discuss. How do we decide which theme to engage with first when they all seem relevant? Usually, I put this question to the client and ask them what they would particularly like to get out of the session. However, I also use my own judgement about what to focus on, guided by my belief in the primary importance of my client's emotional state. My strategy is to identify their *hot spot* – the issue about which they are most emotionally aroused in the here and now of the session.

I do this for two reasons. First, this issue matters to the client even though they might not initially acknowledge or even be aware of this. Through exploring it, we gain valuable insight about their emotional patterns. Second, if the client's feelings of anxiety, anger, excitement, sadness and so on remain unacknowledged and unexplored, they will function as a barrier and reduce the client's capacity to listen, reflect or learn from discussion of other topics. For this reason, I sometimes take the initiative early in the session and direct the coaching conversation down a particular route; on other occasions I begin by following the client's path for a while but will turn down another route if I feel we are missing the hot spot.

Ralph

This latter approach was one I used in a session with Ralph, a senior executive in a multinational energy company. He was in coaching as part of his preparation for succession to the board when his boss retired at the end of the year. Among other things, Ralph was working hard at improving his relationships with senior stakeholders and developing a more motivating style with members of his team.

When we had been working together for a couple of months, Ralph started a session by telling me that he wanted to focus on preparing himself for a presentation he had to make to the board and thinking about the best way to lead a workshop that he was planning for his team. He mentioned in passing that there had been another 'massive blow-up' with Brian, one of his peer colleagues with whom he had a complicated, difficult relationship but added, 'not that I want to go into it – it's too ridiculous!' As we had spent plenty of time discussing Brian in the past, in a rather repetitive way, and as his first two topics were relevant and time-critical, I accepted this at face value and we began to talk about the presentation he had to make to the board.

After a short while, however, I had the sense that Ralph was not fully present in our discussion. Usually lively and open, he seemed distant and disengaged. He also seemed slightly irritated with me, brushing aside a couple of suggestions I made about the forthcoming presentation. I began to think that there was not much I could do to help him and became aware of feeling a bit useless. Initially, I hypothesized that Ralph's behaviour might be reflecting a level of anxiety about presenting to the board that had not been acknowledged. I also wondered if he was using the defence of *projective identification* and unconsciously manipulating me into experiencing the same sense of inadequacy he might be feeling in relation to this task. Yet when I listened to and observed Ralph with these ideas in mind, they did not seem to fit.

Puzzled, I reviewed the first things that Ralph had shared on arriving for the session. I remembered his throwaway remark about Brian and recalled how upset he had become a couple of months ago over another disagreement with this colleague. I began to suspect that this was the real hot spot for Ralph right now. Rather than say so to Ralph outright, and risk him denying it and shutting down the topic, I commented positively on how well prepared he already seemed for his board presentation. I added that he was impressively calm in relation to such an important issue but that I suspected the Brian incident had, annoyingly, managed to get under his skin. It became clear that this was indeed the hot spot.

Ralph responded immediately, confirming that he felt furious with Brian over their latest contretemps and also furious at the fact that it affected him so much: 'Why should I waste more time talking about him instead of more important problems? It's infuriating!' Ralph was certainly present in the room now. In exploring the Brian story, we were able to examine why Ralph became so emotionally affected by Brian and what he could do to calm down and see the issue in perspective.

I also used my own experience of the session to point out what had happened when Ralph had not allowed himself to share the topic that was really preoccupying him. This enabled him to reflect on the need to pay more attention to his own emotions and attend to what was causing them rather than attempting to dismiss or ignore a problem simply because he did not want to accord it any importance.

Intention versus behaviour

With some clients, the main area in which they need to gain insight is the impact on others of their own behaviour. There is a two-part technique for tackling this challenge that I have found helpful on many occasions. The first step is to make a real point of acknowledging that, however inappropriate their actions, the *client's intentions are usually good*. This is usually true in my experience. Typically, poor behaviour results from an excessive focus on task, anxiety about getting the job done, unrealistically high standards, inadequate boundary setting and weak people management skills, combined with a certain lack of sensitivity to the upset and anger that their conduct provokes in other people. It is rarely the case that the individual consciously intends to distress others.[1] Giving credit for good intentions reduces the client's guilt, shame and anger, and greatly increases the chance that they will accept the idea that their behaviour needs to change (see the case study of Sebastian in Chapter 8). Having got alongside the client in this way, the next step involves emphasizing the difference between intentions and behaviour.

Suzanne

This technique worked well with a client called Suzanne, a back office manager in the investment banking sector. She had been sent for coaching to address her brusque and domineering interpersonal style. Despite clear feedback from her line-manager and via a 360-degree survey, Suzanne was indignant, hurt and puzzled by the feedback. She regarded herself, accurately, as an exceptionally hard-working and conscientious executive who put a huge amount of effort into running her department. She saw herself as a firm but fair manager who expected high standards both of herself and her team. She insisted that her aim was always to do the best for the business.

Having empathized with Suzanne's feelings, acknowledged her positive motivation and the value that she delivered to the bank, I made a simple observation. I pointed out that *we judge ourselves by our intentions but others judge us by our behaviour.* I followed this by suggesting that Suzanne put herself in the shoes of one of her junior colleagues (whom she had criticized quite scathingly for a series of small errors) and think through how her behaviour might have appeared and felt. I emphasized my awareness that Suzanne's intention had been to drive this colleague's performance up quickly, in time for her annual review, but pointed out that this was unlikely to be apparent to the individual. In this way, I was then able to focus Suzanne's attention on the consequences of her management style. For the first time, she was given pause for thought.

A strength taken too far

The coach sensed, however, that Suzanne was finding it difficult to tolerate this new awareness that she *had* upset her colleagues, albeit unintentionally. Therefore he followed this breakthrough with another simple but powerful technique. This is an excellent way of getting alongside the client and reinforcing the working alliance, especially when the client is feeling sensitive or criticized. It consists of introducing the concept of *a weakness being a strength taken too far*, followed by illustrations of what this means in practice.

In this case, the coach pointed out that Suzanne's drive, energy and conscientiousness were clear strengths; however, when taken too far, they could lead to an emphasis on getting the task done at the expense of relationships. Similarly, her commitment to high standards and meeting deadlines were also strengths; but taken too far they could lead to colleagues feeling pressurized. He explained that coaching could help her to cherish her strengths while learning to moderate the unhelpful effects of taking them too far.

The aim here is to protect the client's self-esteem and avoid a defensive reaction so that they feel able to accept the need for change. Through *linking* strengths and weaknesses, the coach can emphasize the client's best qualities while presenting the problem behaviours in a clear but sympathetic light. When I use this technique, I usually underline the point by illustrating it with examples from other individuals who have different strengths and concomitant weaknesses. I often include one or two of my own. This helps to drive home the point that we *all* have areas over which we need to exert some control and become more skilled.

> Suzanne found this formulation helpful and engaged with it enthusiastically. It reduced her growing sense of guilt and shame at her behaviour towards her colleagues enough to prevent her from retreating to her earlier position – an angry rejection of the feedback. It proved a turning point in the coaching process.

Using your own experience of the client

I have already described the information we can glean about our clients from their *transference* – the way they relate to us during the coaching process. This provides useful insight, which I usually note privately rather than comment on. However, on occasion, I choose to feed back to the client my experience of something that they have said or done, whether during or between the coaching sessions. It can be an excellent way to get their attention and to expand their awareness of their impact on other people. It is important, as ever, that the coach is sensitive and not critical in the way they convey their experience if it is not to provoke embarrassment, anger or guilt.

> The opportunity to use this approach arose in the case of Suzanne and was helpful in furthering her self-awareness. During scheduling of the coaching sessions, a mistake was made in Suzanne's office and she was told by her secretary that she had an appointment when in fact she did not. On arriving at the coach's office to find that he was not expecting her, Suzanne became irritated and spoke sharply to the coach's secretary, Janet. She more or less accused Janet of being responsible for the error and for wasting her time.
>
> Although Suzanne emailed an apology to Janet later that day once she realized that the mix-up had originated from her own office, Janet was upset by her outburst and informed the coach. This enabled him, at his next session with Suzanne, to mention the incident. He approached it from her angle, saying it must have been stressful and unpleasant for her to have had a wasted

journey and then become irritated with Janet only to feel she needed to apologize later. He suggested that perhaps it would be useful to explore what had happened inside Suzanne to make her react as she did.

By approaching the issue with tact and in a clear spirit of enquiry rather than blame, he was able to help Suzanne gain considerable insight into specific triggers for her outbursts. Through focusing her experience, rather than Janet's, the coach avoided a defensive reaction and left space for Suzanne to acknowledge how quickly she could lash out at others.

Margaret

I also used this technique in a session with a client called Margaret who tended to bottle up her feelings, avoid dealing with difficult issues and then eventually become extremely upset when the emotional pressure grew too great. We had agreed that she would undertake 360-degree feedback to gather more information about how her colleagues perceived her. However, when it came time to launch the process, she came up with one reason after another for delaying the distribution of the questionnaires. When I attempted to contact her about it, she simply stopped communicating by email or telephone and even cancelled a coaching session.

When I finally saw her face-to-face and raised the issue of the much-delayed 360 and her avoidant behaviour, she became angry and upset, revealing that she was worried about the process and had felt that I was pressurizing her. I suspected she also felt bad about not responding to my messages. My experience of Margaret's outburst in the here and now of the coaching session – and of her previous strategy of 'radio silence' – proved extremely helpful to our work together. It provided powerful evidence of her characteristic emotional and behavioural pattern in which she avoided potential conflict and then became upset. Instead of talking to me, she had avoided me. Raising the issue had given us both a new level of insight and enabled us to explore the changes she could make to handle situations like this more effectively.

Helping the client gain insight into others

As well as helping clients gain insight into their own emotions and behaviour, I often draw on the psychodynamic model to help them gain insight into their colleagues. This can be immensely helpful. Many clients tend to take other people's statements and behaviour at face value. Encouraging them to analyse what may be going on for a boss or peer, and to see the world from their emotional viewpoint, can help the client to take things less personally and adopt a more skilful approach. This can transform a difficult relationship.

Malcolm

This opportunity arose with a client called Malcolm, who came into coaching a few months after being promoted to a directorship on the board of a medium-sized company, one of several owned by a large financial services group. The main issue he wanted to tackle related to his boss Tom, the recently appointed managing director, whose behaviour had left him feeling frustrated and confused. Among other things, it appeared that Tom was micro-managing both Malcolm and his peers, changing strategic direction impulsively and avoiding difficult personnel decisions.

Malcolm's response thus far had been to do his best to meet his boss's demands while using indirect, light-touch attempts to encourage clearer and more consistent decision-making. Crucially, he was interpreting much of Tom's behaviour personally, as a sign that he lacked confidence in Malcolm's abilities. When I helped him to gather and analyse the facts around Tom's recent appointment, his personality, background and the pressures on him, a different picture emerged.

Tom had been promoted to MD from a specialist technical role – he was by nature more of a detail than a big picture manager, and he had little experience of general leadership. The Group CEO was pressing him to bring about rapid improvement in the performance of Malcolm's division, which was experiencing difficult market conditions. When I encouraged Malcolm to use these facts to imagine what his boss might be feeling, he realized that he was probably suffering from a high level of performance anxiety and struggling to adapt to the demands of his challenging new role.

This insight freed Malcolm to stop feeling criticized by Tom and to feel much less uncertain and confused. Instead, we began considering what Malcolm could do to reduce his boss's anxiety. This included proactively providing Tom with more information than he really needed, via a weekly update, as a way of helping him feel in control; this quickly led to a lessening of the micro-management. Malcolm also began to be more assertive when Tom tried to change course inappropriately and he took a firmer stand on the need for Tom to deal with a couple of difficult performance issues. It proved to be containing for Tom when Malcolm became clearer with him, and held firmer boundaries, rather than trying to meet his every request and letting his ineffective behaviour go unchallenged. Malcolm found that Tom's behaviour improved significantly as a result.

Monologue to dialogue

I shall end with a technique that I use to reinforce internal and behavioural change. It also helps clients with the important process of *becoming their own coach*. It is particularly useful when a client has gained insight into a long-established emotional and behavioural pattern, understands the need to modify it, but is finding this hard to do.

This obstacle to change often takes the form of an inner voice that controls the client by continually expressing their greatest fear:

- For Adam, the fear of losing control of his emotions and behaviour leads to a lack of passion and authority. His inner voice is always warning, 'Don't lose control!'
- For Clive, the fear of being exposed as a fraud causes anxiety and preoccupation that distracts him from his real work. His inner voice whispers, 'You're not good enough!'
- For Suzanne, the fear of not completing work to the right standard and on time leads her to pressurize her colleagues in an abrasive style. Her inner voice is constantly nagging her to 'Get it done – don't fail!'

My aim is to *lessen the hold* of these undermining and limiting voices. I start by telling the client that we should not waste time trying to silence this voice completely. I say something like, 'It's coming from an old part of you and will always be a part of your life. *However, we can fight back'*. I suggest that the client visualizes themselves as having an *internal dialogue* in which one side is taken by the old negative voice and the other side by a new, more confident, stronger voice. I tell the client that they can learn to mobilize this new voice at those crucial moments when they want to break free of the old pattern and do things differently. I then model the new voice, sitting up straight and using a confident tone. In Adam's case, for instance, the new voice would say something like: 'Oh right – it's that old "don't lose control!" message again … well I know what that's about but it's not going to stop me bringing some emotion and energy to my work relationships. I can stay calm and professional and still express my passion for the business'.

I follow this up by emphasizing that overriding and ignoring the old voice will lead to uncomfortable feelings that have to be tolerated and lived through. Over time, however, as the new ways of thinking and behaving become more embedded, the old voice will quieten down and gradually lose its hold, becoming an old familiar irritant rather than a powerful foe. I usually explain to the client that this *shift from inner monologue to inner dialogue* is an important part of the process of starting to coach themselves. By internalizing and reinforcing the new voice that I have represented and modelled, they accelerate their capacity to manage both their feelings and their behaviour.

In this way, I support the client's ego – the part of their mind that is capable of rational and balanced thought – against their critical superego and, in some cases, against their aggressive urges. The process of demonstrating both voices myself and acting out the dialogue is important. I exaggerate the whiny or angry nature of the negative voice and bring an authoritative and assertive tone to the positive voice. This helps the client to identify with the second voice and internalize it more strongly.

The coaching process

I shall end this chapter with a brief reflection on the coaching process illustrated in this and the previous chapter. As all coaches know, it is by no means a straightforward or easy endeavour. When we begin work with a client, we must focus on establishing trust and rapport. Without this, the coaching relationship will not get off the ground; and if the relationship is not maintained, the coaching will falter and fail. But to create a really powerful connection with the client, we must offer more than a warm presence and a safe space. Almost from the outset we must demonstrate an empathic and insightful understanding of the client's world. Yet insight is not enough either. Through our earliest observations and comments, we must convey our ability to help the client develop new behavioural strategies to meet their coaching goals – and in a form that is rapidly visible back in the workplace. It is the challenge of simultaneously engaging with these tasks that makes coaching such a complex and rewarding activity.

Note

1. The exceptions to this are individuals on the psychopathic spectrum, as explained by Babiak and Hare (2007).

6 Understanding the organizational context

In the previous two chapters, I explored my one-to-one work with clients, which is the focus of this book. Here, I would like briefly to share some further thoughts on the importance of the three-cornered relationship between coach, client and organization – the framework within which executive coaching takes place.

The earliest stage of the coaching process is often when the coach has the best opportunity for learning as much as possible about the client's organization and its dynamics. In my experience, a good deal can be gleaned from the way in which coaching is commissioned and the way in which the organizational stakeholders relate to both coach and individual client in the course of agreeing a coaching programme.

First contact

Most executive coaching assignments begin with a telephone call or email from someone other than the prospective client themselves. Often a member of an organization's human resources, learning and development or talent management departments will initiate contact. Sometimes it will be the line-manager and, on occasion, the would-be client will make contact directly, particularly in the case of the most senior individuals. There is usually an exploratory telephone call with the person commissioning the coaching when the coach is briefed about the organization and its issues, the client's background and role and their coaching needs.

Typically the client and coach are then put into direct contact to arrange an initial consultation, often called a 'chemistry check'. Sometimes it is agreed or expected that the coach will contact the client to organize this meeting, sometimes that the client will contact the coach. Occasionally, the caller wishes to make the appointment on the client's behalf.

This first meeting is designed to help the client decide whether they would like to work with a particular coach – and vice versa. It has become quite common for clients to meet at least two or three coaches so as to make a better-informed decision. As a result, the time between that first contact and the client's decision to go ahead with a coach can stretch over several weeks or even months. The meeting with the client, usually offered without payment, varies a good deal in length and depth, according to the coach's approach, and may or may not lead to an immediate decision by the client. If unsuccessful, the amount of feedback a coach may ask for or be given also varies greatly.

Interacting with the organization

If this pre-coaching process is slow and convoluted, it can be a frustrating experience for the coach. If the coach is keen to gain new work, it will be an anxious period. If the coach has a busy, established practice, it can represent a significant and speculative investment of unpaid time. The competitive element when a client is meeting several coaches brings its own pressures. However, from a psychodynamic perspective, these first interactions with the client organization form an important part of the coaching process. They often provide valuable clues to themes that emerge later on during the work itself. The contrasting experience I had when approached by two different organizations illustrates this.

The manufacturing business

The first was a traditional, French-owned manufacturing business with a hierarchical structure and a conservative approach to management development.

Martine
Following a lengthy telephone conversation to explore my background and discuss the prospective client, I was asked, together with two other coaches, to submit a detailed written proposal outlining how I would approach the coaching assignment. My proposal and one other coach's were given first-stage approval and then sent to Paris to be read by senior managers. A list of questions came back asking for more information on various points. Once I had replied to these, a further six weeks elapsed during which the two proposals were studied and eventually approved by two further layers of senior management in France. Eventually, four months after the first call, the green light was given and the HR director arranged for the client to

meet myself and the other coach. I met the client, Martine, a director of the UK business, she decided she would like to work with me, I agreed and the coaching finally got underway.

The view of the HR director and senior managers was that Martine's main development need was to become more measured and authoritative in her interactions with colleagues, as she tended to come over as impatient and sometimes as irritable and stressed. She accepted these points but, early in the coaching process, described with a great deal of feeling her frustration at having to deal with a complex hierarchy of senior managers, based in France. She felt that they did not always fully understand the UK business yet they insisted on overseeing most of her decisions. She gave examples of the delays and extra work that this caused. Martine was therefore keen to use coaching to work on becoming more skilled at managing upwards, influencing key stakeholders to give her more autonomy, and to cope with the company culture in a way that caused her less stress.

Given her acknowledged tendency to be action-oriented and somewhat impatient, I might well have thought that perhaps she was exaggerating the slow and bureaucratic nature of the organization's culture. Thus, the fact that I had myself experienced this aspect of the organization, as a potential new supplier, turned out to be helpful. It enabled me to be confident about the objectivity of Martine's views and allowed me to focus on helping her understand more about senior management's ultra-cautious approach and find new ways of working more effectively within it.

The professional services firm

This example illustrates the value and relevance of exploring the client's issues, wherever possible, in the context of the wider dynamics that characterize their organization.[1]

Theresa

This client came from a professional services firm with which I had been working for several years. The learning and development manager called me and raised an urgent problem. One of the senior partners, Theresa, needed coaching to help her cope with a demanding new role and a heavy workload. I was thought to be the right coach for the job and she wanted to know how soon I could start. She seemed anxious and I gained the impression that this in part reflected the anxiety of Theresa's head of department, who was apparently 'worried that she might be about to burn out'.

I found it difficult to gain a clear picture of the reasons for the organization's concern and was left feeling anxious about Theresa myself, wondering whether she was indeed close to a breakdown and perhaps needed clinical support rather than coaching. When I had raised this on the telephone, the L&D manager insisted that coaching was the only kind of help that Theresa would accept and that they were sure it was the right thing for her. I went to my diary to find space to see her as soon as possible.

At the first meeting, I gained a different picture of the client and her situation. Theresa was certainly finding aspects of her new role challenging and the workload heavy, especially as she had two young children and tried to leave the office at a reasonable time. However, I felt that she was coping well overall and neither she nor I felt that she needed medical or therapeutic intervention. Instead, two organizational facts emerged.

First, she was the first female partner with children who had been appointed to this level of responsibility, following a case the previous year in which a female associate from another department had taken the firm to tribunal alleging sex discrimination. The case had been settled out of court but had been upsetting and stressful for all concerned. Second, Theresa described her head of department as a well-meaning but stressed individual whose main concern was meeting his departmental targets and who tended to take a hands-off approach to the management dimension of his role. An example of this was his reluctance to confront another partner whose abrasive and inappropriate behaviour towards some of the junior associates was well known. The head of department's own boss, the managing partner, was described as a hands-on, decisive leader who was known for being tough and demanding.

Once again, I felt that the way in which I was approached to coach this client provided me with helpful insights – in this case into how the firm handled anxiety. On the one hand, there was evidence that difficult people problems were ignored until they had become serious. On the other hand, the rushed and slightly panicky way in which I was commissioned to coach Theresa seemed to be an over-reaction. Through sharing these observations in the coaching session, Theresa and I were able to identify and explore the high levels of anxiety – regarding both task and people issues – that currently appeared to exist within the firm. We considered the way in which anxiety was being dealt with and, in particular, noted that it seemed to be unconsciously passed along from one role-holder to another.

Several examples of this were identified, including the chain that led from the managing partner (worried about the risk of another court case) to the head of department (keen to avoid a potentially messy interpersonal situation), to the L&D manager (concerned to support a senior working mother) and on to me. My official role was to deal with this last problem by working with Theresa. At another level, I felt that my role was in fact to contain some of the unacknowledged fears within the system. These insights enabled me to help my client to become much more aware of the unconscious dynamics at play in the firm. This in turn helped her to take timely, thoughtful action to deal with anxiety-creating situations on the one hand and to avoid being caught up in unnecessary panic on the other.

Arranging the first meeting

When contacted by an organizational stakeholder with a view to coaching a particular client, I always suggest that the client or their personal assistant gets in touch to make the appointment. Asking the client to take responsibility for calling or emailing me achieves two things.

First, it acts as a litmus test of the client's feelings about the coaching. If a client delays getting in touch – sometimes despite repeated reminders from the organizational stakeholder – I regard this as pertinent information. It is often an early warning of high levels of anxiety or ambivalence. This is helpful to bear in mind when the meeting eventually takes place. Sometimes persistent delay indicates insufficient agreement between the prospective client and their organization that coaching is the right intervention. This flags up the need for the decision to be readdressed internally before a meeting is arranged.

Second, asking the client to make the first contact with the coach transfers the process into their hands, encouraging a greater sense of ownership and control. This is particularly important when the client has conscious or unconscious fears about confidentiality between the coach and the organization. If the coach and stakeholder jointly set up the initial appointment for the client, this can add weight to the client's impression that they are in close contact, with all that this implies.

Managing the three-way relationship

When a first meeting has gone well and coach and client have agreed to work together, certain steps must be taken to launch the coaching programme. These include agreeing a contract covering logistics, fees, expectations and methods of measuring success. Provisional coaching objectives may be clarified.

My practice is almost always to propose an early three-way meeting between the coach, client and the client's line-manager. This serves to engage the line-manager as fully as possible in the client's development and provides an invaluable opportunity for drawing out their perceptions of the client's strengths and weaknesses. In my view, this is a vital step that ensures alignment around the coaching agenda – or in some cases surfaces a lack of alignment that can then be tackled internally before the coaching gets fully underway.

Both the three-way meeting and the liaison with the HR sponsor also serve to ensure that the key organizational stakeholders feel their perspective has been sufficiently taken into account. During the course of the coaching programme, I liaise with the organization at several key points to gather feedback and share headline coaching themes and a sense of the client's progress – with the knowledge and agreement of the client. I also encourage the client to acknowledge their accountability to the organization by updating their boss and HR partners on a regular basis as to how the coaching is going. Towards the end of the coaching programme, the review and evaluation process involves close liaison with the boss and other stakeholders.

At a psychological level, the executive coach's dual accountability – to the individual client and to the organization that has commissioned and is funding the coaching programme – is not straightforward. I find that to work effectively with my clients, I must be willing to *identify* with their experience and *ally* myself with their interests. Yet at the same time I must also identify and ally myself *with their organization* and the key stakeholders such as their line-manager and HR.

When there is substantial alignment between the two, this task is not necessarily difficult, though maintaining careful boundaries is essential. For example, a good relationship with the HR director involves staying in touch and keeping them informed of progress but this needs to be done in a way that is transparent and agreed to by the client. When there is tension or conflict between the client's needs and interests and those of the organization, I have found myself walking a tightrope – and sometimes falling off.

Paul

An example of the difficulties involved in managing dual accountability arose early in my coaching career when I worked with a young investment banker called Paul. During a brief telephone conversation with a L&D manager, I was told that he needed to build his self-confidence and improve his business development and stakeholder management skills. During the chemistry check, it became clear that Paul was experiencing a great deal of pressure at work and was having difficulty coping despite working extremely long hours. In particular, he was having problems with his line-manager. It seemed that this boss was an impatient and irascible man who continually demanded more work from Paul, frequently criticized him in cutting terms and scarcely ever gave positive feedback. The detailed, specific examples that Paul gave me rang true and I did not feel that he was exaggerating.

While inappropriate behaviour and worse is not unusual in the investment banking world, I felt that Paul – a likeable, unassuming individual – was at real risk of being victimized in a way that was at best unhelpful and at worst dangerous to his mental and physical health. I started to explore with Paul how he might handle his boss more assertively and whether there was anyone in the system to whom he could turn for help, but I did not feel optimistic about his situation and was left feeling angry and concerned on his behalf.

As I had a longstanding relationship with the bank's HR director, who had been on leave when I had been approached, I obtained Paul's permission to share my concerns with her. When we spoke, I found myself feeling angry as I described my impression of Paul's boss's behaviour and critical of the organization for not addressing it. I also worried that I had been asked to coach Paul to help him cope better with a bullying boss and was therefore colluding with a situation in which this behaviour was effectively condoned. As it turned out, the situation was more complex than it had seemed.

It emerged that Paul's line-manager himself was under enormous pressure from a difficult boss – he had been charged with turning round a struggling department and felt that his job was on the line. He had inherited an under-performing team of which Paul was a member and while the boss was seen as having low emotional intelligence, he did not have a track record of explicit bullying. Paul was felt to have potential but was seen as resisting his boss's repeated requests to focus on business development activities. He apparently tended to bury himself in the areas of work that he felt most comfortable in and was taking a passive stance in relation to the challenges facing the department. The more his boss pressured him, the less responsive he became and thus a vicious circle had developed. I discovered that the boss's management style was being addressed and that he had recently started coaching with a view to managing his emotions and behaviour more effectively.

My learning from this episode was that my identification with Paul during the session had gone beyond what was helpful. I had allowed the part of me that is susceptible to being a *rescuer* to be triggered by his account of the situation. While speaking to the HR director to get a fuller picture was a helpful step and overall the conversation went well, I may have given the impression of being too much on Paul's side. From the bank's point of view, the purpose of the coaching was to help Paul raise his performance to another level – or to clarify that he was unable to do so in which case he would be moved out.

It would have been helpful for the organization to have provided me with a fuller briefing about the situation surrounding Paul before I met him, yet it was my responsibility to hold the balance between engaging with Paul's reality and holding in mind the possibility of another, organizational reality. When I went on to have a three-way meeting with Paul and his boss, I was able to help them to have an honest and professional conversation in which some of the difficulties between them were surfaced. While keeping Paul's welfare in mind, I also ensured that he had understood what his boss needed from him, how he needed to change and checked that he was committed to using the coaching to address these issues. This lay the basis for a successful piece of work in which Paul confronted his fears and his unhelpful pattern of passive withdrawal and gradually became more confident and proactive as a business developer and in his relationships with senior colleagues.

As this case illustrates, maintaining the balance between getting alongside our clients and not becoming too influenced by the client's view of the world is not an easy task. Engaging with the client organization at the outset of the process, staying in touch with the key stakeholders throughout and investing in the joint evaluation of progress at the end will pay dividends. Giving these aspects of executive coaching careful thought helps us to manage the essential task of holding the client's work setting continually in mind as we explore their individual dynamics.

Note

1. Although this *systemic perspective* is not the subject of this book, I regard it as a valuable additional perspective (see Obholzer and Zagier Roberts, 1994; Brunning, 2006) and one that also draws on psychodynamic concepts.

7 The Emotional Profiles Triangle

Throughout this book, I aim to show how our emotions shape and reflect our inner landscape and how we evolve unconscious psychological defences that help us to maintain a sense of safety and avoid being overwhelmed by anxiety and other difficult feelings. At the heart of my approach to coaching is the ability to identify what makes a client anxious and how they respond to that anxiety, as this sheds light on those areas in which they will benefit from making a psychological shift.

It is with these points in mind that this chapter introduces a new model, developed in 2010 with the help of Kate Lanz, called the Emotional Profiles Triangle (EPT). We have used it with teams, at workshops and with a wide range of coaching clients. It draws on both psychodynamic concepts and neuroscience and has proved an extremely helpful means of raising awareness and motivating clients to change.

Although the EPT was developed during the recession to help leaders understand and manage themselves under pressure – and this chapter will refer to leadership effectiveness, leadership style and so on – *it is applicable to individuals at any organizational level who have responsibility for others*. Thus, I hope that this model will prove useful to any coach who is interested in the psychodynamic perspective. For those not trained in psychodynamic theory and practice, in particular, it serves to make the approach more accessible. It does this by providing a framework that simplifies and clarifies three underlying emotional and behavioural patterns.

In the next three chapters, which are devoted to client case studies, the EPT will be used alongside other methods and techniques to illustrate its application.

The origins of the Emotional Profiles Triangle

The EPT emerged from my observations during two decades of coaching practice. Working with executives in a wide range of organizations and roles,

I noted that almost all my clients were struggling in one of three specific ways to handle their feelings and behaviour effectively under pressure. Their emotional difficulties primarily took one of the following forms:

- They failed to control their anger.
- They avoided conflict.
- They disengaged emotionally.

Three of my clients, whose brief descriptions opened Chapter 1, are described in depth in the case studies that follow in Chapters 8–10. They provide good examples of each of these problems:

- For **Sebastian**, the coaching issue was learning to control his aggression. When under pressure, he became anxious about achievement and control, projected his own sense of inadequacy onto others and attacked them. This amounted to bullying behaviour that was threatening to derail a promising career.
- For **Daniel**, the coaching issue was learning to deal with conflict. When under pressure, he became anxious about displeasing people, denied his own and others' aggression, avoided confronting problems and rationalized this behaviour. This eroded his effectiveness, making him vulnerable to being a victim and preventing him from developing his leadership authority.
- For **Nicola**, the coaching issue was learning to access and share her emotions so that she could engage more authentically with colleagues and become a leader who inspired others. When under pressure, she repressed her feelings and held rigid boundaries so as to feel in control, at the expense of her own impact.

Through working with these clients and many others like them, I concluded that the three kinds of difficulty were linked to three different patterns of unconscious anxieties, conflicts and defences – what I have called *emotional profiles*. I noticed that individuals with each emotional profile had certain predictable strengths and weaknesses in their roles as leaders of people. They would lead well in a particular way and lead badly in a particular way.

The Emotional Profiles Triangle

It was this that gave rise to the EPT, a model that defines *three emotional profiles, each of which underpins a specific set of closely linked functional and dysfunctional leadership or interpersonal behaviours*. It puts forward the idea that *all* individuals move back and forth along the spectrum between their functional and dysfunctional forms of leadership. The degree of effective and ineffective leadership that they are able to deliver will depend partly on their psychological and emotional health and resilience, and partly on contingent, external pressures.

The aim of the EPT is to provide a bridge between psychodynamic thinking and the executive coaching conversation. It is a conceptual and practical coaching tool. Through understanding and holding the three profiles in mind, the coach is helped to gain a rapid sense of the client's underlying psychological pattern. They can then use the model to help the client gain insight, learn to manage their feelings and behaviour more effectively, and develop or consolidate the most skilled and effective version of their leadership style.

Who is the EPT for?

Most of the clients we see are by definition successful professionals who function reasonably well most of the time. They usually come into coaching to build on their strengths or address a specific area in which they are under-performing. Nevertheless, experience has shown that many find themselves unwittingly slipping into the dysfunctional side of their emotional profile under pressure, with negative consequences for themselves, their colleagues and their organizations. Regardless of whether these individuals are senior executives, middle-managers or 'high-potentials', we have found that the EPT can be helpful, particularly when the client is experiencing challenging times.

It is important to note that some individuals who come to coaching have a more or less permanent default position at the unskilled, destructive end of their emotional profile. These individuals are likely to be prisoners of excessive or rigid defence mechanisms, developed early in their lives, or have other significant psychological conditions and problems. They will probably not be amenable to coaching. The EPT may be helpful in enabling the coach to come to this conclusion.

Three emotional profiles

Figure 7.1 shows the *effective leadership style* that is characteristic of each emotional profile.

Leaders at the top of the triangle

As Figure 7.1 indicates, at their most effective those leaders at the top of the triangle bring *a great deal of emotional, mental and physical energy* to their leadership role. They mobilize high levels of passion, drive and determination and direct these primarily towards achieving the *task*. They are often powerful

Most leaders tend to have one of the following as their primary
(although not exclusive) emotional style:

*High energy, passionate and driven,
they are task-focused and set the direction*

*Warm, inclusive and relationship-focused,
they like building teams and developing
others*

*Calm, cool and collected, they like an
objective, logical, data-driven approach
to the task*

As people mature, they become more able to use all three styles of
behaviour, although they retain their underlying emotional pattern

Figure 7.1   The Emotional Profiles Triangle: three effective leadership/interpersonal styles

and charismatic, respected and admired by their followers. They lead from the front and charge into battle with their standard held high, followed by their loyal troops. At his best, this was **Sebastian**'s style of leadership.

Leaders at the bottom left of the triangle

Those leaders at the bottom left of the triangle, at their most effective, also bring *considerable emotional energy* to their leadership. However, their emotional energy is directed into *relationships* and they are warm and inclusive. Their focus is on delivering what the organization needs through working with other people: building teams, nurturing talent, developing potential. They can be inspirational role models, loved and trusted by their followers. They lead from among their troops, with one eye always on the welfare of the foot soldiers. At his best, this was **Daniel**'s style of leadership.

Leaders at the bottom right of the triangle

Those leaders at the bottom right of the triangle *do not bring a high level of emotion to work*. They are consistently 'cool, calm and collected' – self-contained individuals with a clear and logical focus on the *task*. They can be steady, rational and objective, unflappable in a crisis and respected and relied upon by others. They go into battle alongside their followers, drawing on relevant data and providing direction with understated determination. At her best, this was **Nicola**'s style of leadership.

It is clear that individuals from all three profiles can deliver outstanding leadership and make tremendously valuable contributions to their organizations. As they gain experience and mature, and especially if exposed to developmental opportunities, most leaders will become fairly competent in all three leadership styles. However, each will retain a primary style – the one that reflects their emotional profile, is most fundamental to them and comes most naturally. Executive coaches should aim to help clients understand and hone their primary emotional style while also developing their repertoire to include the skills characteristic of the other two styles.

When anxiety strikes: three dysfunctional leadership styles

In my experience, most leaders are able to demonstrate one of the three effective styles for much of the time, although of course there is considerable individual variation in consistency and skill. It is under the impetus of specific events – or when pressures build up – that the leader's anxiety is triggered and the shift towards the dysfunctional version of their emotional profile takes place. Neuroscience helps us to understand what happens by revealing the physiological basis of our unconscious emotional reactions (Goleman, 1996; Damasio, 2006; Gladwell, 2006). The amygdala, the small almond-shaped area deep inside our primitive limbic brain, reacts to a signal of danger or threat by flooding our bodies with adrenaline and other chemicals. It switches us on to full alert, emotionally and physically. This takes place incredibly quickly, before the rational part of our modern brain is even consciously aware of a problem. Just like the rest of the animal kingdom, human beings respond in one of three ways: *fight, flight* or *freeze*.

These three defensive mechanisms embody the involuntary shift that takes place when an individual moves from the most effective version of their emotional profile to the least effective. When a certain level of anxiety has been triggered, it is the three types of unskilful and destructive behaviours described in Figure 7.2 that seem to be in the driving seat. It is of course the case that at different times and in different situations, all leaders will demonstrate fight, flight or freeze reactions. But the EPT model posits that individuals have a typical reaction – or default position – when faced with threat or under significant pressure, as this version of the triangle illustrates.

Fight leadership – aggression

The task-focused, highly emotional leaders at the top of the triangle tend to go into fight, as their primary reaction to a danger signal or threat is to mobilize aggression. However, this aggression is no longer constructively channelled

Under significant pressure, leaders tend to respond primarily
(although not exclusively) in one of three ways:

*FIGHT: Aggression is mobilized and they fail
to control their anger, which results in critical outbursts,
irritability or powerfully passive aggressive behaviour*

*FLIGHT: Fear is mobilized and they fail
to control their anxiety, which results in passive
or manipulative behaviour and conflict
avoidance*   *FREEZE: Feelings are shut down and they
fail to engage emotionally with others,
which results in a sense of remoteness and
lack of connection*

Figure 7.2   The Emotional Profiles Triangle: three dysfunctional responses to pressure

into driving forward the task. As adrenaline floods their bodies, their capacity to control their emotion is significantly reduced. The main form their anxiety takes is a fear of losing control. This anxiety drives their unmanaged aggression in the direction of other people. It may emerge in a number of forms, including angry outbursts, direct or indirect attacks, excessive criticism, irritability or impatience.

The aggressive behaviour of the leader in *fight* has a powerfully destructive effect. It creates fear, resentment and mistrust among staff, generates a blame culture, a lack of risk-taking and a toxic atmosphere.

Flight leadership – avoidance

The relationship-focused, highly emotional leaders at the bottom left of the triangle tend to go into *flight*, as their primary reaction to a danger signal or threat is fear. They become suffused with anxiety about other people but their concern is no longer constructively channelled into helping people succeed in their tasks. As adrenaline floods their bodies, their capacity to manage their emotion is compromised. The main form their anxiety takes is fear of losing the approval and acceptance of others. This blocks their ability to deal with situations involving conflict or tough decisions. It leads to avoidant, appeasing or self-distracting behaviour in which they abdicate taking difficult decisions in a timely manner or fail to stand their ground on important issues.

The behaviour of the leader in *flight* creates an atmosphere of anxiety, insecurity and a sense of frustration within their organization. Staff may worry that the vulnerable leader needs to be protected, creating an inappropriate role-reversal. Political in-fighting to fill the power vacuum often develops.

Freeze leadership – emotional withdrawal

The task-focused, less emotional leader at the bottom right of the triangle tends to go into *freeze*. Their response to threat is primarily to shut down their feelings. However, this is no longer in the service of a constructive, considered approach to getting things done. As adrenaline floods their body, their capacity to mobilize even a small amount of emotion is reduced. The main form their anxiety takes is fear of being emotionally overwhelmed. This blocks their ability to connect with their own feelings or empathize with others. They become remote, uncommunicative and withdrawn, unable to connect and engage with their staff.

The behaviour of the leader in *freeze* creates uncertainty in their organization because no-one knows what they are thinking, generates frustration and anger as followers feel abandoned, and erodes staff motivation and morale.

Public figures who illustrate the three emotional profiles

A good example of a public figure with the emotional profile at the top of the triangle is Gordon Brown. As Chancellor of the Exchequer and then as Prime Minister, his supporters often referred to the passion, energy and conviction that he brought to his work. His drive and commitment were evident. However, over time, his reputation for aggressive outbursts, relationship difficulties and a domineering interpersonal style came to dominate his leadership. Despite the best efforts of his spin-doctors, his inability to manage his emotions under pressure seems to have played a significant part in his downfall.

Gordon Brown's predecessor as Prime Minister, Tony Blair, illustrates the bottom left-hand profile. Blair is widely regarded as having excellent relationship-building skills and a notable capacity for warmth and empathy. Yet the memoirs and diaries of those close to him that have been published since his departure from office in 2007 emphasize his repeated failures at critical moments to stand up to either Gordon Brown, then the rebellious and subversive Chancellor, or to George Bush. The consequences of what many see as his avoidant and placatory behaviour are still being debated today.

A striking recent example of the bottom right-hand profile is Tony Hayward, former CEO of British Petroleum. An engineer by training, he brought a calm, low-key, rational approach to the role, following the resignation in 2007 of the more volatile Lord Browne. However, in the face of the deep-sea oil explosion in the Gulf of Mexico in 2010 in which 11 people died, Hayward's leadership failed. Crucially, he failed to convey publicly adequate concern about what had happened or to demonstrate enough empathy with those affected by the tragedy. Instead, three months after the disaster, with oil still gushing into the sea, he made the fateful comment that he 'wanted his life back'. It was Hayward's slide into dysfunctional leadership characterized by an inability to mobilize enough emotion, rather than the disaster itself, that made his resignation inevitable.

Regaining effectiveness: the challenge facing leaders with the three profiles

Clearly, the impact of all three dysfunctional styles on the leaders themselves, their staff and their organizations can be enormously destructive. Before describing how coaching can help leaders return to their more functional, skilful selves, the final version of the triangle summarizes the challenges that face each emotional profile (Figure 7.3).

Interestingly, the challenge facing those with each profile involves developing some elements of the skills that are characteristic of the other two profiles when they are at their best. So those at the top of the triangle need to reduce emotion and calm down (like the bottom right profile) and connect with others and show more empathy (like the bottom left profile). Those at the bottom left of the triangle need to become more driven and task-focused (like the top profile) and more objective and less emotional (like the bottom right profile). Finally, those at the bottom right of the triangle need to mobilize more emotional energy and passion for the task (like the top profile) and

To return to their most effective selves,
leaders need to rise to these challenges:

*Those who go into FIGHT must calm down and regain
perspective, reconnect with other people, and show
more empathy and appreciation*

*Those who go into FLIGHT must reconnect
with the task, find the courage to overcome
their fears and be more honest with
themselves and other people*

*Those who go into FREEZE must mobilize
their emotions, re-engage with other
people and the task, and risk sharing more
of themselves*

Figure 7.3 The Emotional Profiles Triangle: three challenges

become more relationship-focused and connected with others (like the bottom left profile).

Using the EPT

The EPT provides an easily understood framework for executive coaches to use when helping clients improve their capacity to remain effective and skilful, even when anxious. My colleagues and I have tested the EPT in numerous workshops and seminars, as well as using it with many senior individuals and teams. In virtually every case, clients have found little difficulty in identifying their own emotional profile.

Occasionally, people are not sure when shown the first version of the triangle, which describes the three effective leadership styles – perhaps because they have developed a good level of competence in all three sets of skills. However, when the second version of the triangle describing the dysfunctional styles is explained, their underlying profile almost invariably becomes clear. Moreover, clients have rapidly identified the profiles of their bosses, colleagues, direct reports and other significant figures in their working lives.

Consistent feedback has confirmed that leaders, and those who work with leaders such as members of the human resources community, have also found workshops and presentations about the model to be useful, especially when there has been the opportunity to begin to explore its application to oneself. That said, it is particularly when working with individual coaching clients in depth that the EPT can provide most value. Its combination of conceptual and behavioural dimensions enables coaches to use it to help clients gain insight, learn to manage their feelings and behaviour more effectively, and deliver more consistently the most skilled version of their leadership style.

Using the EPT with Sebastian, Daniel and Nicola

The three chapters that follow contain the case studies of Sebastian, Daniel and Nicola who were briefly introduced at the beginning of Chapter 1 and again earlier in this chapter. They provide in-depth illustrations of the psychodynamic thinking and practice described in this book and are designed to bring alive the concepts, strategies and techniques that I use with my clients.

These individuals are also good examples of the three EPT profiles. Their stories reveal the typical conscious and unconscious dynamics that characterize the three profiles. Although the EPT was only one of the models and techniques I drew on in my work with Sebastian, Daniel and Nicola, I shall summarize its benefits here, before the case studies, as these are relevant to all coaching clients:

- The EPT enabled me to focus quickly on the key challenge facing Sebastian, Daniel and Nicola through providing a simple three-cornered framework within which to place them. Having identified which profile I thought fitted them best, I was able to use the notions of *fight, flight* and *freeze* as lenses through which to examine and understand their behaviour.
- The EPT then provided an extremely useful way of helping these three clients acknowledge their underlying issues. As the model applies to all leaders, at every organizational level, and as each profile comprises both strengths and weaknesses, it protected their self-esteem and reduced the shame and vulnerability that they could easily have felt had I simply focused on their difficulties. In each case, it helped the client to recognize their emotional and behavioural issue without becoming defensive.
- Critically, the EPT also helped these clients to develop deeper insight into what was happening for them, under the surface, when they moved from the most skilled and effective version of their leadership to the least. This level of understanding made it easier for them to identify the key triggers that pushed them in the dysfunctional direction.
- The EPT also laid the basis for the development of practical new strategies for avoiding these triggers, managing their feelings more effectively when they cannot be avoided, and remaining at their most resourceful and constructive, even under pressure.
- The model also helped motivate Sebastian, Daniel and Nicola to address their challenge with confidence and determination. On the one hand, this was because they could clearly see the pathway between the more and less positive versions of themselves and felt hopeful that they could make progress. On the other hand, they were also spurred on by their growing understanding of the negative effects of their dysfunctional behaviour on their colleagues and organizations.
- These three clients also used the EPT as a powerful but accessible tool with which to think about their colleagues, whether boss, peers, team members or other stakeholders. They generally found it easy to place these individuals at one of the corners of the triangle and benefited from the new insight into other people's feelings and behaviour that the model provided.

I hope that the case studies that follow will also demonstrate the flexibility of the EPT. This is part of its value – it can be easily adapted to best meet the needs of a particular client. Finally, one of the most useful features of the EPT is that it enables the executive coach to identify and work with a leader's underlying dynamics *even when little is known about the individual's family background, upbringing or life experience.* This reflects my belief that it is not always necessary – though where possible it is often helpful – to understand the origins of our clients' unhelpful patterns or rigid defence mechanisms to help them develop and change in depth.

8   The client who bullied

This case study is about a client whose emotional and behavioural pattern illustrates the profile at the top of the Emotional Profiles Triangle (EPT) and whose default position was therefore *fight*. He is a good example of a high-achieving individual whose passion for the task spilled over into aggression against others when he was under particular pressure and unable to maintain himself in a skilful and resourced state.

Key psychodynamic insight

A vital point to remember about the inner landscape of clients with Sebastian's EPT profile is that individuals who tend to be critical or attacking of others when under pressure almost always have a highly critical inner voice that attacks them in a similar way. This explains why, despite the hurt they inflict on others, this is often not their conscious intention. Their subjective experience is usually that of angry victim. This must be addressed, alongside the impact of their behaviour on others, if they are to be helped to change this pattern and move back into the most effective version of their EPT profile.

The client

For **Sebastian**, executive coaching was effectively imposed from above. An able and ambitious lawyer in his late thirties, he was a rising star in the litigation division of a leading City law firm. He had joined his firm as a salaried partner a year before coaching started and had a successful track record as a fee-earner and a growing reputation within his particular field. He was popular with his clients and was extremely good at business development. Only one aspect of his performance was threatening to damage – or even derail – this promising career.

The main coaching issue

I first heard of Sebastian when I received a call from the HR director of his law firm whom I knew well. She told me that they had a serious problem relating to the behaviour of a partner whom they valued highly. Sebastian was a lateral hire, recruited one year before from another firm and offered partnership. When I asked what qualities had led to his recruitment, she said that Sebastian was bright, determined and an excellent technical lawyer who performed consistently well on client deals. His working relationships with senior colleagues, peers and, usually, with other staff were generally good, particularly with those whose intellect he respected, and he had developed some close professional friendships with two or three of his peers. These factors, combined with his successful approach to business development, had initially led to expectations of a glittering future. So what had gone wrong?

It emerged that Sebastian had been the subject of a number of informal complaints since quite shortly after his arrival and the term 'bullying' had been used on several occasions. It seemed that when Sebastian felt that junior colleagues or support staff were under-performing or had made a mistake, he behaved in a way that was unacceptably aggressive. This ranged from sarcastic remarks and irritability to withering criticism. He had on several occasions shouted at individuals, sometimes in the open-plan office. There was general agreement that this behaviour took place mainly when Sebastian was under stress, usually in the midst of a client deal. When I asked for an example, the HR director described a recent incident when, following an all-night session spent preparing papers for a client, Sebastian had discovered a careless error in a piece of work done by a young associate named Kevin. Had this error gone undetected, the firm would have been seriously embarrassed. Sebastian went to find Kevin at his desk in the open-plan office and shouted furiously at him in front of colleagues, calling him an idiot and swearing.

The head of litigation had given Sebastian feedback about his conduct in the past but it seemed that the message had not been conveyed with sufficient impact. It had been met by Sebastian with defensiveness and half-hearted agreement that he would 'try to stay calm' but he had mainly complained about the pressure he was under and the shortage of competent associates within the team. His behaviour had not noticeably changed. The final straw had been the resignation of a secretary who cited Sebastian's outbursts as one reason for her departure.

Sebastian's head of department had decided that this situation could not be allowed to continue. He consulted with the managing partner and the HR director and they had called Sebastian to a formal meeting. The seriousness of his behaviour was spelled out to him and it was made clear that his future in the firm, and certainly his chances of becoming an equity partner, depended on dealing with this problem. Sebastian had apparently responded with a mixture of anger and distress. He had attempted to play down his behaviour, blaming it on the overload and the stress of client deals, while maintaining that he was sorry if anyone had been upset. He was shocked at the possible consequences for his future and argued that there were equity partners in the firm whose behaviour was much worse than his. But the senior managers were adamant and repeated their message. When coaching was proposed as a means to help him change his behaviour, Sebastian reluctantly agreed. He was asked to contact me to arrange an initial meeting.

Preparing for the first meeting

It was two weeks before Sebastian's secretary contacted my office to arrange an appointment. Before our first meeting, I reminded myself that Sebastian would, almost certainly, be feeling ambivalent or outright hostile to both me and the coaching process. According to the HR director, Sebastian had acknowledged but not fully accepted the firm's view of the problem and no doubt felt aggrieved at being compelled to address his behaviour in this way. Given the circumstances, I expected that he would be feeling anxious, humiliated and angry.

The coaching challenge

The challenge I faced was how to gain Sebastian's trust while not colluding with his denial of responsibility for his unacceptable behaviour. I would have to achieve the right balance between empathizing with Sebastian's experience of the situation and confronting him with the need for change. If the coaching was to be effective, he would have to recognize that he had behaved in a way that had seriously upset a number of colleagues. Yet if he experienced me as a critical, judgemental figure, his defences would stay up and a working alliance would not develop.

This tension was not unusual but the fact that Sebastian had been effectively compelled to enter coaching made it particularly acute. I reminded myself of my own susceptibilities – both the anger that bullying aroused in me and my tendency to identify strongly with the client's view of the world – to prepare myself for remaining in role and holding the centre ground in what was bound to be a difficult session. I was also aware that there was likely to be an additional challenge with a client like Sebastian, namely the need to pass an unspoken intellectual test. With his high-flying academic and professional track record, it would be important that he experienced me early on in the process as someone he could respect and who was worth taking seriously. Rather than explain my own credentials, I planned to address this issue indirectly through the insights that I would bring to our discussion.

Containing anxiety

When Sebastian arrived at my office, I saw a tall, good-looking man in his late thirties. He had considerable physical presence and I gained an impression of intensity and nervous energy. As we settled into the coaching room and I offered him refreshments, his face and eyes conveyed quick intelligence and some wariness – he was on his guard. Behind this, I sensed some anxiety and vulnerability and this helped me to warm towards him.

Rather than asking Sebastian to open the conversation, I decided to begin by raising the difficult circumstances surrounding our meeting and outlining what I had been told. I felt that this transparency would reduce his anxiety and have a containing effect while ensuring that the seriousness of his situation was surfaced from the start. I said that I was glad to meet him but appreciated that he might have mixed feelings about being here. I proposed telling him what the HR director had told me and then hearing his thoughts and feelings about the situation. I emphasized that the content of our conversation was confidential, although we would both need to share with the firm our views on whether the coaching should go ahead. I then outlined the content of my briefing, including the behavioural issue, the formal meeting and the consequences for his future should this problem remain unresolved.

Framing the problem: avoiding a defensive reaction

When referring to Sebastian's behaviour, I was keen to avoid a defensive reaction and wanted to make it as easy as possible for him to acknowledge the problem. Therefore, I deliberately used language that softened the impact of the message a little while not avoiding it, such as: 'I gathered that, especially when you are under pressure in the middle of a deal, your sense of urgency and determination to deliver can lead to frustration with junior staff. I can understand that. The problem seems to be that the way this urgency and frustration is expressed sometimes lands badly and upsets people. Though you may be 100 per cent right in what you are asking for, and may not intend to upset anyone, it sounds as if there has been some collateral damage on the relationship front and it is this that is now coming back to bite you.'

To avoid adding to Sebastian's sense of humiliation, I did not dwell at this stage on the impact of his behaviour on those at the receiving end. I did stress, however, my understanding that the firm was taking this issue seriously and that there was a good deal at stake. I finished my summary and made a point of anticipating some of his feelings, both to show empathy and to make it as easy as possible for him to express them. I said something like: 'I can well imagine that you might be feeling angry, shocked and hurt by what has happened. Clearly, you are extremely able, and the firm has told me how much they value your contribution. Yet your commitment, hard work and successful track record have not prevented this crisis. I know that being sent to see a coach to "get fixed" never feels great.' I then invited him to explain to me his own understanding of the situation.

As I had been speaking, I could see by Sebastian's reactions that my approach was working reasonably well as he relaxed a little and nodded his head at several key points. Although he looked uncomfortable when I described the problem behaviour, I felt that I was just managing to avoid triggering a defensive reaction. Sebastian then shared his views on what had happened. Unsurprisingly, perhaps, he focused on the formal meeting, which he felt was hugely unfair and had been badly handled and was an over-reaction to 'a few petty complaints from poor performers'. He felt that they should have approached him directly rather than complaining behind his back.

I listened carefully and neither agreed nor disagreed. I asked him whether, leaving aside for the moment how it had been handled, he felt that there was any substance at all to the allegations of inappropriate behaviour. I was pleased to find that Sebastian was able to acknowledge that he did get stressed during deals and yes, he probably did react too sharply when things went wrong and perhaps that did upset people sometimes. Although he quickly reverted to complaining about how unfairly *he* had been treated, I felt that he had shown a flash of honesty and insight about his own behaviour on which we could build.

Making sense of the client: developing a working hypothesis

Reflecting on what I had heard and seen so far, I felt clear that Sebastian's default position when under pressure was *fight*. What I needed to understand in some depth was what exactly drove this reaction to such a marked and repeated degree. As I thought about what he had said – the amount of work that he took on, his commitment to his clients, his concern about quality and meeting deadlines – together with his intense, emotional style, I began to develop a working hypothesis about what lay behind his aggressive behaviour. In forming this view, I recalled the HR director's firm opinion that Sebastian was 'essentially a decent guy'. I also drew on my experience of similar clients and my emotional response to Sebastian during the session. Alongside his fury, I had sensed real distress at the idea that he had hurt others.

My hypothesis was that a major factor fuelling Sebastian's outbursts was his difficulty in paying sufficient attention to his own needs. Specifically, he did not seem to be setting appropriate boundaries around the amount and level of work that he took on. A perfectionist, he placed himself under enormous pressure and aimed to control or check every aspect of his team's work to make sure it was meeting his high standards. When the pressure grew too great and he became exhausted, his anxiety about his own performance and his frustration at not getting everything done became too much to bear. Instead of being able to channel his aggressive energy into tackling the *task*, it erupted inappropriately towards *other people*, usually triggered by evidence of under-performance on their part.

At the same time, Sebastian's excessively conscientious behaviour and huge workload was leading to a build-up of resentment in him towards the firm as a whole, including senior colleagues whom he felt were unsupportive or not pulling their weight. I guessed that angry questions arose in his mind when he was particularly stressed. Why was he working so hard when others were not? Why was his contribution and commitment to the firm not recognized and appreciated? Why would some of his colleagues not put in the effort needed to get things right? When external pressures became too great, it was this combination of performance anxiety and what could be described as a sense of *angry victimhood* that drove Sebastian's aggressive behaviour and lack of empathy towards others.

This hypothesis led me to the view that, unfortunate as his behaviour undoubtedly was in the heat of the moment, Sebastian was *not* a systematic bully whose aim was to hurt and humiliate others. Rather, he was a driven, somewhat insecure perfectionist who was failing to manage his own needs and boundaries and who experienced overload as a danger signal to which he responded with *fight*. When this happened, he lost his capacity to empathize with others and felt that his behaviour was justified, although he did feel quite remorseful later. His bullying, I felt, took place despite not because of his attitude towards other people, which was essentially well-meaning.

Separating the person and the behaviour

To test this hypothesis and to position myself firmly *alongside* rather than against Sebastian, I made an intervention designed to drive a wedge between the *person* and the *behaviour*. Having listened at length to his account of what had taken place, I said with some energy that there was one thing that seemed clear to me: 'While I think we might both recognize that your behaviour under pressure is not working well, you strike me as a person who does *not* get up in the morning and set off to work planning to upset other people. This is clearly not your intention at all. In fact, my guess is that you feel bad when this happens and are appalled at the idea that you might have upset a junior colleague enough to reduce them to tears.'

This was a turning point in the session. Sebastian nodded and seemed near tears himself. He said that this was absolutely true and that one reason he had been so upset by the formal meeting is that he was being accused of bullying when in fact he hated bullies and was horrified by the idea that he could be seen in this light. My sense was that his emotion and words were entirely genuine. I acknowledged how upsetting the current situation must be.

By identifying Sebastian's good intentions so explicitly, my aim was to drive a wedge between his underlying character and his inappropriate behaviour, while not denying that the latter existed. Through acknowledging that he was fundamentally a good person and not a bully, I wanted to protect his self-esteem and reduce the feelings of guilt and shame generated by the firm's actions and his own critical inner voice. My intervention was also designed to strengthen that part of Sebastian that wanted to change and to build our working alliance. I wanted him to feel that he and I were on the same side and that our common enemy was his inappropriate behaviour and the stressful conditions that had generated it.

Building the working alliance

To continue building trust, and encouraged by his response, I went on to demonstrate my concern for the part of Sebastian that was being victimized by his current approach to work. I proposed that we use the coaching process to examine closely whether he was taking sufficient care of his own needs, as well as helping him stop his outbursts. I said I could see that his commitment to high standards led him to drive himself extremely hard. This had played a crucial part in his professional success, yet I suspected he was paying a high price by not protecting himself well enough against excessive demands. This price included behaving under pressure in a way that upset others – and was now getting him into trouble too. Finally, I expressed optimism about the chances of coaching being helpful. I was confident that he could learn to make some significant changes to his working patterns, find better ways of coping and manage his feelings more effectively. This would enable him to avoid the irritability and angry outbursts that were proving so problematic.

This opened the door for us to begin the process of exploring Sebastian's underlying emotional dynamics with a view to bringing about significant and sustainable behavioural change. Alongside Sebastian's willingness to take some responsibility for his behaviour, I was encouraged by his response to me, which I could feel was shifting from suspicion and resentment to engagement and trust. He seemed less tense and anxious and I felt that a combination of empathy with his feelings and intentions, and honesty about the seriousness of the problem, had helped him to feel more contained. These early steps in our interaction laid the basis for the work that was to follow.

High achiever, low self-esteem

In our second session, Sebastian provided some brief but helpful information about his background. The second son of two successful parents – his father a lawyer, mother an academic – with a bright, sporty older brother, Sebastian was a high achiever from an early age. His parents emphasized scholastic excellence and Sebastian described his father as a volatile man who became easily irritated and, while devoted to his sons, could be critical and scathing at times if they failed to live up to his expectations.

While we did not explore Sebastian's early life in depth, what I learned shed some helpful light on his inner world. The expectations and pressures of his family environment, combined with Sebastian's innate drive, his ability to succeed and the praise he received as a result, all reinforced his determination to achieve. However, they also seemed to have reinforced his tendency *to value himself primarily on the basis of his achievements. This led to an underlying insecurity about what he was truly worth without them and a deep-rooted fear of failure.* The strategy that Sebastian developed to defend himself against the painful anxiety that the risk of failure evoked was to throw himself into his work and do whatever was necessary to ensure that his record of success was maintained.

How well did this strategy serve Sebastian? On the one hand, he reaped rewards in the external world, achieving good academic results and progressing rapidly in his career. On the other hand, he struggled truly to internalize and enjoy his achievements. He was pleased and relieved to get excellent A level results, for instance, but such successes made little true impact on the self-critical, insecure part of himself that was always waiting in the wings. This meant that he was vulnerable to a collapse in self-esteem if things went wrong.

I offered these thoughts to Sebastian more or less as I have described them here, making sure that I did so with empathy and in a spirit of enquiry. I prefaced the points I made by mentioning the inevitable impact on all of us of parental role models and family expectations. I also carefully observed Sebastian to see how my remarks were being received and to check that they were making sense to him and that he was not feeling defensive or alienated. In fact, he responded positively and expressed relief that I had both understood and gone some way to explain his insecurity and low self-esteem – problems he knew he had but found difficult to share, or even to admit to himself, and impossible to explain at a rational level.

Sebastian then built on what I had been saying by sharing a further episode from his past – his unexpected failure to get into Oxford University. While this would be disappointing for most people, Sebastian described how for him it had been a devastating blow to his self-confidence and self-esteem. Listening to him, it was clear to me that this failure had triggered painful feelings of worthlessness and shame as well as loss. Prey to the condemning voice of his superego, he saw his rejection as confirmation of his fears that he was not really as good as others believed. Although Sebastian had tried to rationalize what had happened by blaming Oxford's alleged prejudice against pupils from private schools, the main impact of the episode was to reinforce both his determination not to fail again and his vulnerability to low self-esteem. From then on, even when failure was only a possibility, the threat would be enough to fuel his anxiety and trigger his defences.

Why now?

Having understood more about Sebastian's background and its influence on the emotional and behavioural patterns that he had developed, I began to wonder what might have happened over the past year or so to fuel his aggressive behaviour. When a client comes into coaching in crisis, as he had done, and we begin to explore the problem, I always ask myself the question, 'why now?'

To understand what had precipitated Sebastian's current difficulties, I asked about his experience at his previous and current firms. In particular, I wanted to gain a sense of how he had coped with stress and pressure before and after his move and promotion to partner. An interesting picture emerged. It seemed that Sebastian had consistently done well at his previous firm where he had spent six years as a junior and then a senior associate. His description of his pre-partner career confirmed the picture of an ambitious, task-focused individual who brought a good deal of passion and emotional and physical energy to work each day. As I now knew, Sebastian had a strong psychological need to succeed and it appeared that this was underpinned by a structured and organized approach to his work. It seemed that, at his old firm, his characteristic strategy of long hours combined with close control of his assignments had worked well. As a promising young lawyer, he had successfully focused on delivering what partners and clients asked of him. Impatient to become a partner himself, he moved to his current firm rather than wait for partnership where he was.

The transition to the new firm and partnership had clearly been a difficult one. It turned out that his current organization had a culture that was less aggressive than that of his old one, with more emphasis placed on good interpersonal skills and respect for colleagues. Most significantly of all, he faced an entirely new set of expectations now that he was a partner. He was shouldering a different level of responsibility and he would be accountable if something went wrong. He also needed to provide value for the firm by leveraging the work of associates, as well as through his own client work. Therefore, he was expected to direct, motivate, coach and monitor a team of younger, less experienced people and ensure that they delivered results. This significantly reduced Sebastian's sense of control over the outcome of his work and created greater dependency on others. He felt more accountable yet less secure in his ability to perform and impress.

As he described these changes, I could see Sebastian becoming quite upset. Before my eyes, he was experiencing some painful emotions as he acknowledged how challenging and difficult this past year had been for him. He admitted that it had affected his confidence, and his enjoyment of work, much more than he had realized. When I suggested that his new role as partner had brought with it a heightened risk of failure and therefore a powerful threat to his sense of self-worth, he agreed. As before, he was clearly relieved as well as distressed to be surfacing and examining the feelings he had been pushing out of conscious awareness.

Sebastian's pattern of defences

We went on to explore in more detail exactly what Sebastian was finding most difficult in his current role. It did not take long to clarify this – when he was responsible for the successful outcome of a fast-moving, complex and high-value client deal, his feelings of stress and anxiety became acute. He deployed his usual strategy, namely to work even harder and exert an even higher level of control over the task. However, to deliver a successful outcome, he was forced to rely on junior associates and support staff, some of whom he did not deem competent. *This created a level of pressure within Sebastian that his usual strategies failed to deal with effectively.* When faced with a trigger such as a mistake – or even a possible mistake – on the part of a junior colleague, he experienced an emotional cocktail of anxiety, loss of control and anger that boiled over.

Emergency measures

At this point, I suggested that we take some time to address the immediate issue of how he could stop these outbursts from occurring, even though it would take time for us to understand and address the underlying causes. Sebastian was keen to do this as well. The shock of being confronted about his behaviour meant that he was extremely anxious about doing anything else that could conceivably be described as bullying. We therefore focused on identifying some immediate steps that he could take when he felt the familiar emotions building up. These included breaking eye contact, using a breathing exercise and leaving the room if necessary and walking round the block to calm down. This helped Sebastian to feel more secure but it was clear to me that these were only emergency measures that I hoped would control the problem in the short term while we worked to change the dynamics behind it.

Sebastian's defences: projection and identification with the aggressor

Before describing more about the coaching process itself, I shall share my understanding of the unconscious dynamics that underpinned the dysfunctional sequence of events that Sebastian was caught up in. Specifically, which defence mechanisms was he using, when under most pressure, in his attempt to retain a feeling of psychological safety? It seemed to me that in those moments when Sebastian turned on a colleague he was using *projection* – transferring the part of himself that he felt was intolerably inadequate and stupid onto the person concerned, whom he then castigated harshly. At this moment of highest emotional arousal, Sebastian's resentment at the long hours and huge effort he put into his work allowed him to feel *justified* in lashing out, as if *he* was the victim. This served temporarily to block the empathy and concern for others that he would usually feel.

I felt that the example the HR director had given me of Sebastian's fury with his junior associate Kevin was particularly telling. Kevin's mistake had been one that could have shown Sebastian and the firm in a bad light in the eyes of the client. The threat of being shamed in this way must have fuelled Sebastian's anxiety to unbearable levels, given his insecurity and his reliance on avoiding failure at all costs.

As well as using projection, I discerned another psychological defence mechanism in Sebastian's behaviour – *identification with the aggressor*. This is a dynamic that sometimes develops when a child is regularly at the receiving end of aggressive or critical behaviour by an adult. All children are of course strongly influenced by the role models that their parents or other significant figures provide. But a child who experiences parental behaviour as an attack may attempt to reduce their anxiety, pain and vulnerability by identifying with the strong, powerful attacker. In some cases, the child concludes, consciously or unconsciously, that all relationships involve a power struggle and a winner and loser, in which case it is better to win than to lose.

In Sebastian's case, when he felt particularly anxious and out of control, he found himself adopting his father's scathingly critical style. This was despite the fact that he had been the victim of it himself and, at a conscious level, strongly disapproved of this approach. In these moments, Sebastian's identification with the aggressor – combined with his psychological need to project his intolerable feelings of inadequacy onto others – drove what amounted to bullying behaviour.

What happened after Sebastian's aggressive outbursts or critical attacks? While he usually calmed down quite quickly, those on the receiving end were naturally left angry, hurt and upset. Sebastian was not insensitive to this, and did experience remorse, but he tended to rationalize his behaviour and move quickly on to the next task rather than reflecting deeply on what had happened or making amends. He used the fact that he was pushing himself harder than anyone else to justify to himself his short temper and sharp tongue. He assumed that his colleagues would realize the pressure he was under and would understand that everything he did was in the service of the task. It is this that helps explain why he was so genuinely shocked and distressed when confronted by the firm with accusations of bullying.

In light of this pattern of behaviour, it seemed to me that the main work of the coaching would be to help Sebastian stop victimizing himself – and therefore others – so that he could realize his full potential as a gifted professional and leader.

Key coaching tasks

After my second session with Sebastian, I took stock and reviewed our first two meetings. Despite the difficult start, I thought that the basis had been laid for a strong working alliance with enough trust and engagement from Sebastian for our work to be effective. I also felt I had a good understanding of what was driving his unacceptable behaviour. My main aim now was to find the best way to develop his own insight and to help him learn to manage his internal and external pressures in a different and more constructive way. However, I did not expect this process to be easy or straightforward. For Sebastian to break the destructive pattern of excessive effort, exhaustion, resentment, anxiety and aggression and to modify the defence mechanisms that drove this pattern, he would have to accomplish some significant developmental tasks.

The key coaching tasks as I saw them were to help Sebastian to:

- Set firmer boundaries around himself and his work to reduce his constant experience of overload and the consequent fatigue, stress and resentment. This involved paying more attention to his own needs, asking for help when necessary and learning how to say no (to colleagues and clients) in an appropriate and considered way.

- Manage his anxiety and anger more effectively through becoming more aware of what triggered these reactions.
- Develop strategies for anticipating and avoiding these triggers where possible.
- Cope better when avoidance was not possible through embedding techniques for remaining calm in the moment, even when his anxious and angry feelings were aroused.
- Change his attitude towards colleagues whose performance did not match his expectations through understanding much more fully the impact of his behaviour and the damage it caused to the individual and to their relationship.
- Start feeling better about himself through understanding and confronting his feelings of insecurity and low self-esteem. Crucially, this would make him less vulnerable to self-critical attacks and therefore less likely to project his own sense of inadequacy onto others.
- Stop identifying with the aggressor through understanding this dynamic. Consciously he did not want to be a bully, so accepting that there was a part of him that did indeed behave in this way would be painful but necessary if he was to break the pattern. He would have to tolerate the feelings of shame and guilt that would come with this understanding.

Using the Emotional Profiles Triangle to develop insight

With these goals in mind, I set about developing Sebastian's self-awareness. It is important to note at the outset that in my discussions with Sebastian I did not at any point use technical terms such as *projection* or *identification with the aggressor* when exploring what might be going on under the surface of his conscious mind. While the concepts of psychological defence mechanisms were invaluable in helping me make sense of his dynamics, the language I used was designed to build a bridge between his understanding and my own.

It was in this context that I decided to introduce the EPT to Sebastian at our third coaching session to help him gain insight and engage with the coaching tasks. In taking him through the model, I explained that all of us, particularly those carrying leadership responsibilities, tended to have one of three main ways of handling emotions at work. I described the three categories, with equal emphasis on the positive and negative aspects of each one. Predictably, given his issue, Sebastian did not take long to identify himself as falling into the group at the top of the triangle.

As a model that applies to everyone, the EPT serves to normalize the idea of a less effective default position and makes it easier for the client to accept this side of themselves. This proved particularly helpful with Sebastian, who was struggling to deal with his feelings of guilt, shame and embarrassment in the wake of being accused of bullying. With my active encouragement, the EPT enabled him to make a critical reassessment of himself. On the one hand, his self-perception improved as he saw the link between his leadership strengths and his bad behaviour and understood the latter as something he did under pressure rather than as a reflection of his true character. On the other hand, because he felt better about himself and was therefore feeling less defensive, he was more able to recognize and acknowledge the true impact on others of his aggressive behaviour, something he had previously played down. This represented a breakthrough upon which the rest of the coaching process went on to build.

Using the Emotional Profiles Triangle to promote change

The EPT also proved useful in motivating and encouraging Sebastian to make the necessary behavioural changes at work, along with the underlying internal shifts. The part of the model that outlined the specific challenge that leaders with each profile faced in regaining their best selves helped him to crystallize what he needed to do differently. He found the idea of developing an approach that drew on the strengths of the other two profiles particularly appealing. He identified two senior colleagues whose leadership styles he admired, one from his old firm and one from the current one, and whose profiles were (1) cool, calm and collected and (2) people-oriented and empathic respectively. Sebastian decided to use them as role models and to focus on developing his ability to remain more objective and more empathic under pressure, without losing his hallmark drive and passion for getting things done to a high standard.

Identifying these individuals with different profiles from himself helped Sebastian in another way too. He admired them but could also see the less effective and skilful sides of each of their profiles. The cool, calm and collected colleague could become remote and distant in a crisis and the people-oriented, empathic colleague did have a tendency to avoid difficult interpersonal situations and sometimes failed to take tough decisions. This enabled Sebastian to see more clearly the particular strengths that he brought to his leadership at his best – enthusiasm, energy and a determined focus on delivering results for the business.

Monologue to dialogue

One of the ways in which I helped Sebastian challenge his persecuting superego and control his reaction to a junior colleague's mistake was the technique called *monologue to dialogue* introduced in Chapter 5. I characterized Sebastian's old inner voice as saying something like, 'He's such an idiot, can't he do anything right?!' at the moment when his anxiety and anger had built up to intolerable levels and he went into *fight*. The new voice that I modelled reinforced Sebastian's objective understanding that this reaction was neither helpful nor fair. The new, constructive voice said something like, 'OK, here comes my automatic response – and it *is* incredibly frustrating when something goes wrong! But I'm going to breathe, calm down and contain my urge to lash out so that I can take a more balanced and considered view before responding.' This worked well and was an important element in consolidating Sebastian's inner shift and developing his own *inner coach*.

Setting boundaries

My focus on coaching Sebastian to take responsibility for meeting his *own needs* also played a crucial part in the successful modification of his old destructive pattern. I persistently encouraged him to set sensible boundaries around his working hours, manage his clients' expectations more proactively, prioritize his work more ruthlessly and delegate more to his associates. He began to take steps in this direction though this felt excruciatingly uncomfortable as they raised his anxiety levels. However, with great courage and perseverance, he stuck with this strategy, which gradually became easier as he found it led to positive rather than negative consequences. Just as importantly, Sebastian began gradually *to identify with the attitude of care and concern for him that I was modelling* and as a result to feel less condemning and more nurturing of himself.

A different way of holding others to account

One aspect of taking care of Sebastian's own needs was learning how to manage his associates effectively. He made a great deal of progress through our work on how he managed a colleague called Rosie. This was a junior associate whom Sebastian found consistently annoying and with whom he had lost his temper on two or three occasions in the past. His description of her left me feeling that she probably was a poor performer and not easy to manage. However, Sebastian's behaviour towards her had made things worse.

Crucially, when we examined the history of his working relationship with Rosie, it emerged that Sebastian had failed from the outset to address her poor performance, telling himself that it would be a waste of time as she would not improve. Behind this lay a fear of getting too angry with her or of laying himself open to criticism for handling an associate badly. It had just seemed easier to complain about her to others and do some of her work himself. Rosie had of course picked up his non-verbal irritation with her, which further reduced her motivation and confidence.

In one of our coaching sessions, Sebastian decided to arrange a meeting with Rosie at which he would clear the air by apologizing for having lost his temper with her on the earlier occasions. He would then outline his expectations of her work as explicitly as possible and bring specific examples of areas in which her performance needed to improve as well as a couple of examples of where she had done well. He prepared carefully beforehand and was able to communicate calmly and clearly with Rosie in a way that was new. His apology did clear the air – they both felt better afterwards – and his more specific approach to her performance got her attention. This became the first of a series of regular meetings between them, which continued to go well with Sebastian remembering to acknowledge the improvements that Rosie was making while reiterating firmly what he expected from her. Where she needed more help, coaching or guidance to achieve her goals, he now made time available to provide this.

Over the following months, we worked together on these themes. Sebastian's self-awareness increased rapidly. Of course, understanding himself better did not mean that he could easily set aside his painful feelings about himself or his tendency to externalize these feelings through blaming others – this took time. However, Sebastian's sense of self did steadily improve, along with his ability to acknowledge his inappropriate behaviour and his confidence that he could do things differently in future.

Outcome

In due course, we gathered feedback about Sebastian's behaviour and impact from key stakeholders and, later, from the wider team via 360-degree feedback. He was generally perceived as being much calmer and more managed in his leadership style. He was now seen to be dealing with junior colleagues in a professional and appropriate way. Several specific examples of change and improvement were fed back.

Over the course of a year, meeting every four weeks, Sebastian continued to make progress and to consolidate the internal and external shifts needed to transform his performance. His sense of self-worth, his capacity to set boundaries, his ability to address problems with colleagues in a calm and timely way and to manage his feelings had all significantly improved. When our work came to an end, his key stakeholders within the firm were delighted and his prospects of promotion to equity partner looked excellent. For both of us, it had been a challenging but ultimately extremely rewarding journey.

9   The people pleaser

This case study is about a client whose emotional and behavioural pattern illustrated the profile at the bottom left of the Emotional Profiles Triangle (EPT) and whose default response was therefore *flight*. Daniel is a good example of a warm and enthusiastic individual whose natural focus on building relationships led to difficulties in dealing with conflict and poor performers, especially when he was under pressure.

Key psychodynamic insight

A critical point to remember about the inner landscape of clients such as Daniel is that those individuals who could be described as 'too nice' are often fearful of aggression and deal with this by denying their own and other people's negative feelings and behaviour. This leads to a number of problems. They may avoid addressing difficult interpersonal issues and fail to stand up for themselves. Moreover, when under pressure, their own aggression may emerge in disguised forms – expressed either against others in indirect, usually unconscious ways or internally against the self.

The client

Daniel came into coaching as a result of his line-manager's suggestion and with the support of his HR director. A senior operations director within a large pharmaceutical company, aged forty-four, he had worked in the pharmaceutical sector throughout his career, moving to his current organisation three years previously to take on a more senior management role. Daniel delivered satisfactory if not inspiring financial results in his area of the business. He was seen as a hard-working and conscientious team player and was universally liked. At a recent appraisal, Daniel's overall performance was considered good but some key areas had been identified as in need of improvement.

The main coaching issue

Daniel's line-manager provided a thorough briefing. Having noted his strengths, he told me that Daniel found it difficult to deal effectively with poor performers. He illustrated this by describing the struggle that Daniel was having with a particularly challenging individual within his team. He also explained that Daniel was perceived as lacking authority and leadership impact. He wanted him to develop more influence within his peer group and more gravitas when dealing with top management. He was supportive of Daniel, describing him as a 'lovely chap', and clearly regarded him as a valuable contributor. However, he believed that Daniel lacked confidence and undersold himself.

Due to the success of some of the products in Daniel's area of the business, his team was expanding and his role becoming a more important one within the company. This added some urgency to the need for Daniel to raise his profile, become more decisive and more able to take tough decisions and increase his overall leadership impact. These were the factors that had led his line-manager to propose coaching as a way for Daniel to address these issues. Daniel was reported as having responded positively to this idea. Three days later, he contacted my office to arrange a first appointment.

Preparing for the first meeting

Following this briefing, I reflected on how Daniel might feel at our first meeting. I guessed that he might be quite self-deprecating and keen to get on well with people. Recommended by his boss, I might well represent an authority figure in his eyes. He had seen my biography but did not know me, nor did he have any experience of executive coaching. I thought it likely that there would be some anxiety about what the process would involve and particularly about how I would see him. What had his boss said to me? Would I judge him critically? Would I want to work with him? I suspected that he probably would keep these worries to himself and be accommodating and friendly.

The coaching challenge

The main challenge I anticipated with this client related to Daniel's 'niceness', a strength that seemed likely to be the source of some weakness as well.

I would have to establish a working alliance that provided enough containment and safety for him to trust me with his vulnerabilities and enough challenge to take him out of his safety zone so that we could explore some of his fears and inhibitions. I guessed that it would be quite easy for me to connect with and support Daniel but that motivating and enabling him to become more assertive would be difficult.

Drawing on my experience of other clients with the *flight* EPT profile, I suspected that to achieve this Daniel would need to grapple with a fear of becoming 'selfish' and unpopular. This would mobilize his fear of conflict and also present a serious threat to his 'nice' self-image, which was likely to be a major source of self-esteem.

Containing anxiety

Daniel arrived fifteen minutes early for our meeting and was apologetic when our office manager let him in and settled him in the waiting room. When I came down to find him, I saw a man of medium height with curly light brown hair and a pleasant, open face. He jumped up to shake hands and smiled. He seemed a little nervous and began telling me about his journey and how much quicker it had been than expected. I found myself liking him and, sensing his anxiety, greeting him with particular warmth.

As we settled into the coaching room and I poured him some tea, Daniel made friendly small talk and was quick to nod and smile. I sensed some nervousness in his on–off eye contact and a slight eagerness to please. He thanked me for making the time to see him and joked rather unconvincingly that he was looking forward to 'being under the microscope'.

When we were settled, tea in hand, I told Daniel that his boss had called me and given me a little background about him but that I was keen to hear from *him* how I might be able to help. With Sebastian, who had to contend with the humiliation of having been sent for remedial coaching, I had decided to start by telling him exactly what I knew so as to surface the painful topic of his bullying behaviour and make it clear that I was keen to hear his side of the story. With Daniel, however, I felt his anxiety would dissipate more quickly if he started to speak, so I gave him the initiative and put him in control of setting the scene.

Daniel nodded enthusiastically at my suggestion and launched into a detailed account of his career history, his current role in the pharmaceutical company and some of the issues that he was facing at work.

Identifying patterns

Observing and listening to Daniel, I formed the picture of a warm individual who enjoyed his work and showed good empathy with his colleagues. He talked about his team, for whom he seemed to feel a strong sense of responsibility, and how hard his people had been working over the past six months to develop the successful production and distribution of an important new medication for high blood pressure. He expressed his positive regard and respect for his boss and was appreciative of the support that he had received from him. He seemed more ready to praise others than to advertise his own strengths.

When I asked him about his coaching goals, Daniel mentioned that he would like to get the best out of his direct reports, including one individual whom he felt he was not handling well, and to improve his influencing skills. He was also keen to become a more confident presenter. When I said that his boss had raised the issue of developing his leadership authority and making more impact at senior levels, he acknowledged this but seemed less enthusiastic, wryly commenting that achieving this might be 'quite a tall order'. When I gently probed further, he said, with some feeling, that he did not like company politics and would not want to become like some of his peers who seemed to put their own agenda and career before the good of the business.

These comments struck me as interesting and led me to reflect on what might be going on in Daniel below the surface of his conscious mind. At one level, I suspected, he was understandably afraid of failure – of trying to become more authoritative and finding that this was impossible. However, I was more intrigued by the emotional energy with which he had commented on his peers. His voice and words had conveyed a critical quality – suddenly Daniel had not seemed so easygoing and tolerant after all. As all human beings have aggressive impulses, I am always alert to where and how this emerges with clients, like Daniel, who are uncomfortable with their own anger.

I developed the working hypothesis that Daniel, by equating authoritative leadership with being political and self-seeking, was defending himself against the discomfort and anxiety he felt around competing with his peers. By linking these two things, he was *rationalizing* his reluctance to address the issue. This rationalization served to justify his own stance and throw doubt on the need to change, while also enabling him to retain the moral high ground. In the context of EPT, this can be seen as a form of *flight* in the face of his boss's expectation that he step up his performance and leadership impact. I wondered whether this defence was also unconsciously designed to guard against an unwanted, disowned part of himself that was in fact quite competitive and ambitious.

Avoidance of conflict

To gain a better understanding of Daniel's perspective and behaviour, I asked him to tell me more about Gerhard, one of six managers who reported directly to him and whom he found particularly challenging. It emerged that Gerhard was a Swiss national in his early thirties who was spending eighteen months in the UK on secondment from the company's head office in Zurich. Daniel described him as bright, hard-working and conscientious. However, it had become clear that the members of the more junior team that Gerhard was managing were unhappy with his leadership style. They found him demanding and quick to criticize; apparently he spent little time with them one-to-one and gave virtually no positive feedback.

Daniel became quite animated while outlining Gerhard's shortcomings, giving several examples of his behaviour and the negative impact this was having on the morale and performance of his people. As I listened to the description of Gerhard's heavy-handed approach to managing his staff, I began to feel increasingly indignant on their behalf – and also a little impatient with Daniel. I found myself thinking, 'this sounds awful so what have you done about it?'

When I asked what Daniel had done to address this problem, he shifted uncomfortably in his chair and broke eye contact. He said that he had tried to speak to Gerhard about his behaviour on two occasions. These conversations had had little impact and he felt that Gerhard was simply not open to understanding the need for change and perhaps not capable of behaving differently. I enquired further about the details of these conversations and it became clear that Daniel had taken an indirect and roundabout approach.

On the first occasion, he had asked Gerhard how he thought things were going and then, when Gerhard said 'fine', not challenged this view. Instead, he simply spoke positively about Gerhard's team members and said that they responded well to lots of encouragement, hoping that Gerhard would take the hint. He did not. On the second occasion, following further feedback from one of Gerhard's reports that a team meeting had gone particularly badly, Daniel tried to be more direct. He suggested to Gerhard that he might take a more inclusive approach to his team, asking for their views on key issues and helping them to feel more engaged and appreciated. However, when Gerhard responded defensively and insisted that he was trying to engage his team members but they were resistant and slow to come up with ideas, Daniel had let the matter drop.

The second difficult situation at work that Daniel talked to me about related to a peer colleague, Amanda, who was head of another area of the business. Her behaviour, as he described it to me, sounded competitive and undermining. Among other things, she had taken sole credit for a joint piece of work they had undertaken, having proposed that she should present their findings at a special meeting with top management. At team meetings, Daniel felt that she was dismissive and critical of his ideas.

Daniel described Amanda's behaviour and its impact in a matter-of-fact way. Perhaps because the victim in this situation was himself rather than a member of his junior staff, he was less animated than when describing Gerhard's behaviour. He also avoided saying anything directly critical of Amanda. When I asked how he felt about what she had done, he said that she was the better presenter and had probably done the right thing for the project by taking the lead. Her behaviour at team meetings was 'just her style – she is really passionate about the issues and I shouldn't really overreact'.

While Daniel said that he found working with Amanda difficult, and would like to improve their relationship, he insisted that he did not feel angry. I was not surprised to hear that he had not confronted her directly about her behaviour, taking the view that raising these things would make the situation worse. He preferred to remain pleasant and professional in the hope that she would respect that approach and become more collaborative in time.

Listening to Daniel talk about both Gerhard and Amanda, I was struck by the extent of his *flight* in the face of potential conflict. I was interested to note that he became quite animated when describing their problematic behaviour, especially in the case of Gerhard's management of his team. Yet when it came to addressing these issues directly, Daniel's energy drained away and he seemed to regard them as entirely outside his control.

Using the counter-transference

I was keen to try and make sense of what was going on for Daniel at a psychological level. In listening to the accounts of his interactions with Gerhard and Amanda, I experienced some strong emotions and found that tuning in to these counter-transference reactions was extremely useful. Most noticeably, Daniel's description of Gerhard and Amanda's behaviour had left me feeling annoyed with both of them. I was struck by the fact that I, who had never met them, seemed to be feeling crosser about their behaviour than Daniel himself. This reminded me that people who are uncomfortable with their own aggression often manage to express their anger indirectly through unconsciously manoeuvring others into experiencing it on their behalf.

On reflection, I thought that this subtle process was indeed taking place in the session. When Daniel finished telling me about Gerhard, I decided to contain the irritation I was feeling and instead confined myself to empathizing with Daniel's concern, commenting that it must be frustrating for him to see Gerhard mishandling his team in this way. *Daniel immediately responded by saying that perhaps he had overstated the problem*, as Gerhard meant well and his behaviour probably reflected cultural differences. I was struck by the way in which Daniel drew back from his complaints about Gerhard the moment I had got close to agreeing with him, as if he was fearful of having been too harsh or unfair. This was an important early indication of how uncomfortable he felt with the critical, judgemental side of himself and how concerned he was about not being seen in a bad light.

Rather than argue my point and risk Daniel becoming more defensive – and because I did not want to take on the anti-Gerhard role – I acknowledged his point about cultural differences. In fact, I went further, mentioning how difficult it might be for Gerhard to adjust to a new language, environment and organizational culture. Interestingly, Daniel nodded briefly but *then re-emphasized the counterproductive effect that Gerhard's behaviour was having on his direct reports*, as if to prevent my being too understanding of his difficult colleague.

This led me to hypothesize that Daniel was experiencing an uncomfortable internal conflict about Gerhard. He did feel angry and critical of him on the one hand it seemed, but frightened and guilty about having these feelings on the other. Therefore, he unconsciously lured me into agreeing with the angry side, which he then promptly disowned. Clearly, Daniel felt scared of his own aggression, perhaps fearing that if he acknowledged it at all, it would go too far. He also seemed scared of being perceived as critical or unsympathetic. Possibly he was also afraid of Gerhard's potential retaliation if he were to confront him. The result was that Daniel swung back and forth, complaining about Gerhard just enough to evoke my support and then, when I expressed it, making a rapid retreat. In relation to Amanda, the pattern was repeated. I commented on her apparent passive aggressive behaviour towards him and he immediately insisted that this might be an exaggeration and in any case it was best to rise above it and not confront her.

Alongside this dynamic, I experienced two different feelings towards Daniel himself. On the one hand, I liked and felt rather protective towards him. His niceness and apparent helplessness had activated the 'rescuer' part of me and I wanted to help him stand up to his colleagues and confront their behaviour. On the other hand, I also felt a sense of irritation with Daniel and a wish to shake him into action. He reminded me of the notion of the powerful victim who evokes frustration in others by complaining about their problems but being determinedly unwilling to address them.

A final element of my counter-transference responses to Daniel in our first session was also interesting. I had felt subtly criticized by his response, early in the session, to his boss's wish that he develop his leadership impact. He was clearly uncomfortable about this idea but expressed his feelings indirectly. As we saw, he used the strategy of linking the concept of leadership impact with something clearly negative – people who are excessively political and jockey for position – which he could then reject from the moral high ground. I was left feeling slightly wrong-footed for having apparently implied that he should engage in such distasteful behaviour. Again, I felt this fitted the theme of Daniel's unconscious aggression emerging but only in the most roundabout of ways.

Building the working alliance

Although I began to develop these working hypotheses during my first session with Daniel, I felt that his level of self-awareness in relation to his own feelings was low. To build a working alliance, it was essential that I moved at his pace. While he was fairly open about not liking conflict much and preferring it when people got on well, he seemed unaware of the extent to which he feared his own and other people's aggression. At this stage, therefore, I decided to tread carefully and made a deliberate choice not to ask him directly why he had not dealt with Gerhard more firmly or stood up to Amanda.

In Sebastian's case, it had felt vital to acknowledge that his fundamental intentions towards other people were good despite his aggressive behaviour. In Daniel's case, I felt that it was vital to show him that I recognized and respected the things he regarded as most important and that were central to his positive self-image. So as the session drew to a close, I told him that I had enjoyed getting to know him and could see that he was a caring, values-driven leader with a deep commitment to treating other people well. I added that it would be essential for him to remain authentic and true to himself whatever changes he might choose to make in the course of the coaching.

While I was acutely aware of the need for Daniel to modify his approach to handling difficult relationships at work if he was to become more effective, I felt convinced that pushing this issue before a strong foundation of trust had been built would be counter-productive. Daniel responded positively to my comments. I sensed his pleasure at my recognition of his values and his relief that I was not going to try and railroad him into transforming his leadership style. He told me he looked forward to working together.

Helping the client own his feelings

At our next session, Daniel told me that there had been some further problems with Gerhard and that he would like to think through how he might tackle the issue. Although encouraged by this, I was keen to avoid a replay of the conversation we had at the first session in which Daniel had denied his anger. I thought there was a real risk that I would fall into the trap of pushing for a firmer approach with Gerhard (which I did indeed think was necessary) only for Daniel to retreat into his passive, helpless stance.

For this reason, I decided to try and raise Daniel's self-awareness in a way that would encourage him to begin to own his negative feelings. I used a technique I call *mixed feelings*, which was described in Chapters 4 and 5. This involves articulating both sides of the inner conflict that one suspects the client is experiencing. The key to doing this successfully is conveying the sense that *both sets of thoughts and feelings are natural and understandable*. This functions to reduce the anxiety, embarrassment, shame or guilt that one set evokes in the client, and encourages and enables the negative feelings to emerge into conscious awareness and be acknowledged.

I told Daniel that I would like to share some reflections on what he had told me about Gerhard. I said that the situation struck me as a really tricky one, as it put him in something of a dilemma. On the one hand, he clearly wanted to support Gerhard and was sensitive to the pressures he was experiencing in his new environment. On the other hand, he was understandably concerned and somewhat frustrated by Gerhard's unskilful management behaviour and its impact on junior staff. I chose this mild wording carefully in the hope that Daniel would be able to accept the point without a defensive reaction. I was delighted when he readily agreed with this formulation and said he realized he probably did need to explore how to deal with Gerhard a little more firmly.

Daniel's defences: repression, denial and projective identification

Before describing the rest of this session, I would like to highlight the underlying dynamics driving Daniel's acute fear of conflict, which was preventing him from dealing appropriately with his colleagues. This can be understood from a psychodynamic perspective through the *unconscious defences* that he was using to retain a sense of psychological safety and protect himself from painful feelings.

So what were these defences? First, Daniel seemed to be *repressing* a whole aspect of himself – those emotions relating to aggression, frustration and resentment – into the unconscious part of his mind. Second, when other people's behaviour stirred up angry or critical feelings despite this, he used *denial* to push them away. But anger is a natural and inevitable part of the human emotional spectrum and repression or denial does not mean that it vanishes altogether. Instead, it goes underground, only to surface in disguised form. This can fuel a vicious circle in which the more the individual represses their aggression, the more frightening and powerful it feels unconsciously, which increases their resistance to acknowledging it.

The other defence mechanism that I identified in Daniel as a result of my counter-transference responses is called *projective identification*. While projection enables people to export an unwanted aspect of themselves and see it in other people, projective identification goes further. It engages the other person by subtly *evoking their identification with the unwanted feelings that are being exported.* Thus when listening to Daniel, I began to feel angry with Gerhard and Amanda, rather than simply thinking that their behaviour sounded unskilful or inappropriate. Yet when I expressed this feeling, however mildly, Daniel immediately took the opposing stance, playing down the very difficulties he had just been describing and disassociating himself from the emotions that they triggered.

It seemed to me that the main driver of Daniel's defence mechanisms, and the fear of his own anger, was his anxiety about being disliked or rejected. Regardless of what other people actually thought of his behaviour, he would feel both guilt and shame if he perceived the slightest risk that he had behaved badly. Equally importantly, Daniel gained a significant sense of self-esteem and self-worth from feeling that he had behaved kindly and patiently.

This illustrates the point already made about anxiety presenting itself in disguised form. Consciously, Daniel had become adept at rationalizing his avoidant behaviour. Although anxiety lay at its root, he did not *appear* overly anxious either to himself or to others.

I suspected that Daniel's defensive pattern, as with most of us, stemmed from a combination of his own temperament and genes and his upbringing, particularly his parents. When I found a good opportunity to ask a little about his background in our second session, I gathered that Daniel's father was rather emotionally remote from his only son and preoccupied with his own interests. Daniel described his mother as loving but a 'worrier' and lacking in self-confidence. Neither parent liked arguments, expressions of anger were not encouraged within the family and tensions or disagreements were generally not surfaced or resolved. The family motto seemed to have been 'Least said, soonest mended'.

Daniel's defensive pattern had developed early it seemed, and had become entrenched over his lifetime. Like many people who are 'people pleasers', Daniel had unconsciously decided to allow behaviour such as Gerhard's and Amanda's to go unchallenged despite the problems they caused him and others. Consciously, he recognized the inappropriateness of their conduct but perceived it as something that he could do little or nothing about. This enabled him to justify his failure to address the situation, achieve a sense of psychological safety by avoiding conflict and retain a sense of himself as a good person who was not aggressive or judgemental.

How well did these defences work for Daniel? At one level, they worked quite well as he had been able to achieve considerable success at work by using his positive interpersonal qualities and his business skills. However, they also exacted a significant price, since he suffered considerable stress as a result of the behaviour of Gerhard, Amanda and others. Just as importantly, their unchecked behaviour had a negative impact on the ability of Daniel's wider team to achieve their organizational goals.

From a career perspective, Daniel's inability to be assertive threatened to limit his progress and I sensed that he had reached a professional crossroads. Although his boss was supportive, he clearly wanted Daniel to address the issues that had been identified and I felt that this was essential if he was to prosper in his current organization. The question facing me now was how to help Daniel raise his performance to the next level. For coaching to be successful, Daniel would have to relax his defensive pattern and make inner changes that would maintain his self-esteem while releasing a more powerful leadership style.

Key coaching tasks

In Daniel's case, I felt that his underlying fear of aggression and his need to please would have to shift significantly if he was to step up to the level of leadership that was expected of him. I saw the most important coaching tasks as helping him to:

- Become more aware of and acknowledge his angry and critical feelings rather than repressing, denying or projecting them. To do this, he would have to learn to tolerate the acutely uncomfortable anxiety and guilt that these feelings provoked.
- Learn that he could choose whether and how to act on his negative feelings – acknowledging them did not mean that they would take control.
- Become able to express his own needs and wishes clearly and honestly in a firm but fair manner. An important part of this would be Daniel understanding the negative consequences for himself and others when he did not do so.
- Build his underlying sense of self-worth and confidence. He had to learn to see himself as a manager who was *both* caring and kind, and capable of setting boundaries and confronting inappropriate behaviour when necessary. This would give Daniel the self-respect and sense of inner authority he needed to take up his leadership role more effectively and with greater impact.
- Learn practical strategies for communicating assertively with colleagues at all levels. This would involve preparing and practising the key messages that he wanted to convey so that they carried conviction and were taken seriously – without becoming aggressive. He needed to ensure that his verbal and non-verbal communications were consistent and authoritative.
- Improve his communication and presentation skills so that they would reflect his increased confidence and authority.

Using the Emotional Profiles Triangle to develop insight

With these underlying tasks in mind, my first concern in coaching Daniel was to shift his focus from the external factors that he felt he could do little to influence – Gerhard's cultural differences, Amanda's dominating style and so on – to himself. Only by understanding and becoming accountable for his own part in these difficult interpersonal situations would he be able to begin tackling them differently.

As with Sebastian, I found that the EPT model was helpful in raising Daniel's self-awareness without triggering a defensive reaction. The most valuable way in which the EPT helped my work with Sebastian was by reducing the shame he felt at his unacceptably aggressive behaviour. This blocked his ability to learn to tolerate his own – and thus other people's – weaknesses more successfully. In Daniel's case, it helped my work in a different way. Here its main value was nudging him into acknowledging his *flight* behaviours. As long as Daniel remained in denial about this, he would remain in his comfort zone, bemoaning problems but not taking responsibility for doing something about them, and nothing would change.

When I introduced the EPT, I focused at the outset only on the effective, skilled versions of each of the three profiles. Had I gone straight to explaining the ineffective, dysfunctional sides, I felt I would have risked Daniel feeling too criticized and becoming defensive. Therefore, I asked Daniel to think about which of the three positive profiles fitted him best. He thought carefully about this and identified the relationship-oriented leader on the bottom left of the triangle.

I then went on to explain the aspect of the model that suggested that, when under threat that could take the form of one big event or a more general area of anxiety, we all moved into a less effective, skilful and resourced version of our profile. In the case of his profile, his relationship-orientation, empathy and excellent interpersonal skills led him to attempt to maintain harmonious relationships and to avoid conflict even when objective reality made this unrealistic, indeed impossible. I did my best to describe this in a way that normalized it and linked it as strongly as possible with his strengths so as to protect his self-esteem while introducing the idea of *flight*.

Fortunately this worked well. I had built a strong working alliance with Daniel, based on a good deal of affirmation and empathy, as well as careful listening to his issues. This enabled him to acknowledge much more fully than before his tendency to avoid recognizing or addressing difficult interpersonal situations even when this was clearly needed. This was a breakthrough that allowed the main work of the coaching to begin – helping Daniel to make a shift in his underlying emotional landscape that would free him to behave differently.

Using the Emotional Profiles Triangle to promote change

As with Sebastian, the EPT also proved extremely useful in helping Daniel to focus on the need for change. By framing his empathy, warmth, capacity to build relationships and develop others as fundamental aspects of his best leadership style, the model helped to affirm this central and highly valued part of his identity. By *linking these qualities to the flight reaction*, which Daniel increasingly recognized and acknowledged, the EPT helped him see that doing things differently did not have to make him unkind, unfair or a 'bad' person. He began to feel safe enough to contemplate the possibility of new behavioural strategies that would allow him to deal more effectively with Gerhard and Amanda. By the end of our third session, Daniel declared himself willing to experiment with changing his approach, a major step for such a conflict-avoidant client.

It is important to note that the way in which I used the EPT to help Daniel accept the need for change and the way I used it with Sebastian were different. In Sebastian's case, having reduced his shame at his bullying behaviour, I appealed to his perfectionism and innate wish to demonstrate the best side of his leadership rather than his worst. With Daniel, having reassured him by reinforcing the fact that the best version of his leadership incorporated the qualities he valued most, I made it safer for him to address the worst version – 'niceness' taken too far, or *flight*. I also appealed to Daniel's concern for others by underlining the negative consequences for his colleagues and his organization, as well as himself, of being unable to deal with conflict. Gerhard's team members were suffering as a result of Daniel not managing his performance; and by not standing up to Amanda, Daniel's whole area of the business was not getting the credit it deserved. I also pointed out Daniel's importance as a role model and the need for his younger colleagues to be able to respect as well as like him.

Finally, the EPT was helpful in providing a focus for the change that Daniel was now willing to engage with. The idea that he could add something of the best versions of the two profiles that were not his appealed to him, as it had to Sebastian. Daniel decided to try and bring more of the enthusiasm and emotional commitment that he brought to his relationships to the *tasks* facing him at work, as those at the top of the triangle did. He also decided to develop the capacity to take a more detached, objective and unemotional view of interpersonal situations on occasion, like those at the bottom right of the triangle.

Gradual progress: surfacing Daniel's negative feelings

Having engaged with these aims, Daniel made steady progress in the coaching sessions that followed. I used several different strategies and techniques to help him achieve his emotional and behavioural goals. In the course of our discussions, we returned to Daniel's family background, his parental and professional role models and some key events in his adult work life. But we focused primarily on his current challenges at work. I concentrated on moving back and forth between helping him develop insight into his own emotions, thoughts and behaviours on the one hand and generating practical new steps that could be applied immediately on the other. These were reviewed and modified as we went along.

From a psychodynamic perspective, the main challenge remained Daniel's conscious fear that he would have behaved badly if he took a firmer approach with others and his unconscious fear of his own aggression. I worked hard to help Daniel accept that he too had the full range of human emotions including anger, critical thoughts and so on. This remained a threatening notion for him and I found myself using the *mixed feelings* technique that had worked well in our second session in relation to a number of specific issues. Slowly but steadily this was effective in helping Daniel accept and become acclimatized to the reality of his own negative emotions.

The behavioural spectrum breakthrough

To address Daniel's resistance to the idea of a plan for increasing his influence and standing within the senior management group, I used a variation of the behavioural spectrum technique introduced in Chapter 5. This was designed to help him visualize his fear of 'flipping' from his old behaviour to the extreme, unacceptable and frightening opposite and challenge it through highlighting the reality of a modest, managed shift. I decided to try this while we were discussing how Daniel could raise his profile as an up-and-coming leader of the business. He was once again expressing his reservations about not wanting to be seen as the sort of highly political person whose only agenda was his own career. Despite my pointing out more than once that raising one's profile and being highly political were not the same thing, this fear was proving difficult to dislodge.

I drew a long horizontal line on the whiteboard and wrote the words 'Highly political and self-seeking' at one end. At the other end I wrote 'Naïve and compulsively self-deprecating', pointing out that this was in fact the direct opposite of the first description. This gave Daniel real pause for thought. As we talked, he had a moment of powerful insight in which he realized at last how his fear of being at one end of this spectrum was trapping him at the other end, which was itself not a constructive place to be. We explored what description he would like to give his own position and came up with 'Honest, authentic, with integrity' and placed it quite close to the centre point on the side that led to the "Naïve" end of the scale.

This allowed us to go on to discuss what new behaviours Daniel could try that passed the 'honest, authentic, with integrity' test and he took the decision to make two changes at the senior management meeting he was attending the following week. One was to engage verbally at least once in each discussion topic, even if he did not feel that what he had to say was absolutely essential or original. The second was to speak a little more fully than usual about what his department had achieved over the past month when it was his turn to update the others. Normally, he confined himself to key facts and figures; now he planned to describe in more detail *how* one of his managers had generated particularly good results through innovation and excellent teamwork. I was very pleased that Daniel seemed to have released himself from his inhibition and was proposing such positive steps.

We applied the spectrum technique to Daniel's attitude to Amanda, too. I put 'Aggressive, competitive, undermining' at one end of the scale and 'Appeasing, placatory, ingratiating' at the other and suggested that we discuss what 'honest, authentic, with integrity' would mean here in terms of his behaviour. He decided that 'fair, friendly if possible, firm if necessary' would be a good description. Although Daniel felt quite anxious at the idea of setting boundaries with Amanda to protect his own needs and rights, he committed himself to trying it. As they were due to manage another joint task, complete with presentation to senior management the following month, we agreed that this provided the perfect opportunity for Daniel's new approach. He decided to arrange a meeting with Amanda ahead of time to clarify how they were going to work together and to communicate what was important to him and how he would like issues addressed. Despite considerable anxiety in the run-up to this meeting, Daniel carried through his plan, including getting Amanda's agreement that he would lead the presentation on this occasion as she had on the last. He was relieved and delighted when this went well.

Outcome

As this breakthrough indicates, Daniel proved able – over a period of six months – to make excellent use of his coaching experience. His progress in raising his profile was further assisted through two sessions with the Sandler Lanz communications coach who specializes in voice and body work. She was able to help him convey more authority and impact through his voice, breathing and posture. This change was clearly visible when I saw Daniel next; he seemed to be standing straighter and conveyed more energy and confidence.

Perhaps Daniel's greatest achievement, after a couple of false starts, was using Gerhard's annual appraisal to deliver a clear and unequivocal message about the need to make changes in his management style. Daniel did this in a way that still felt sufficiently kind and empathic yet left his direct report in no doubt as to what was expected. Despite Gerhard's defensive response, Daniel remained firm and repeated his message with conviction until he knew he had been heard. He asked Gerhard to prepare an action plan for engaging and motivating his team members and told him that the two of them would meet one-to-one every week for the next two months to review this plan and for Daniel to provide coaching and guidance. At my suggestion, he also included the management behaviours he wanted Gerhard to develop in his official objectives, along with specific measures of success.

At the three-way meeting with Daniel and his line-manager before our last session, Daniel's progress was confirmed. His boss described Daniel as demonstrating more confidence and gravitas at senior management meetings and taking a significantly more active role in discussions, including those on wider business issues and not just those concerning his area of operations. Apparently the CEO had also made an unsolicited comment to this effect.

When I asked Daniel's boss about the Gerhard situation, he replied that this no longer appeared to be a problem. He knew that Daniel had used Gerhard's appraisal to address his management style and followed this up with coaching. Although Gerhard's improvement had not been striking, he was coming to the end of his secondment and the main point was that Daniel had called him to task.

I felt extremely proud of my client as I listened to this feedback. Difficult and painstaking as it had been, it seemed that our work had enabled this decent, bright and enthusiastic individual to free himself from some of the anxiety that kept him in a state of ineffective, passive 'niceness'. His emotional profile meant that, under pressure, *flight* would remain his default position and conflict would never be something he found easy. Yet the changes that had taken place internally had allowed him to realize far more of his potential. Much of the energy that he had been using to deny his own and other people's aggression was now available for more constructive purposes. A confident, self-respecting and authoritative leader had emerged.

10 The ice queen

This case study is about a client whose emotional and behavioural pattern illustrates the profile at the bottom right of the Emotional Profiles Triangle (EPT) and whose default response under pressure was therefore *freeze*. Nicola is a good example of a calm, analytical, objective leader whose naturally unemotional style led to difficulties in creating powerful interpersonal connections at work.

Key psychodynamic insight

A critical point to remember about the inner landscape of clients such as Nicola is that individuals who find it hard to engage emotionally are often hiding a sense of vulnerability. They tend to be anxious about being overwhelmed by their own or other people's feelings and maintain a sense of control by keeping them at arm's length. This makes them intensely private and difficult for people to get to know. Under pressure, they tend to become more remote and disengaged just when more connection with their team may be needed.

The client

Nicola was a successful leader in the financial sector who contacted me directly three weeks after her return from the Harvard Business School Senior Leadership Programme. She had been given my name by a former client of mine whom she knew outside work. She explained that she was the managing director of the UK division of a multinational financial services company, a role she had held for five years. At the age of forty-seven, having delivered excellent results in her part of the business, she was one of two possible internal successors to the CEO of the Europe, Middle East and Africa (EMEA) region of the company who was to retire the following year.

The Harvard Leadership Programme had been proposed by the HR director of EMEA as a development opportunity, and Nicola had enjoyed the intellectual stimulation and interacting with a high-powered peer group. However, the programme had included a comprehensive 360-degree feedback process that had gathered perceptions of Nicola by twenty of her work colleagues and this data had highlighted a significant area of weakness in her leadership profile.

The main coaching issue

Nicola had received outstanding feedback about her strategic and analytical capacities but her colleagues at all levels were less positive about her interpersonal abilities. The questionnaire respondents acknowledged that she was courteous and professional in her dealings with others but found her lacking in warmth, hard to get to know and insufficiently available or approachable, especially when under pressure.

She was also perceived as not having much interest in people management. Direct reports said they would like her to spend more time with her team, sharing her experience and providing coaching and more regular feedback. They also wanted her to deal more proactively with poor performers. Finally, several respondents mentioned that when Nicola was stressed, she became more distant than usual and tended to disappear into her office, emerging only to demand detailed information from colleagues that left them feeling simultaneously micro-managed and ignored. Several people commented that they wished she would ask for more help when she was under pressure rather than trying to shoulder the burden entirely by herself.

As a result of this feedback, Nicola decided to seek coaching. She was determined to improve her abilities in these areas partly because she recognized that this issue could make the difference between success and failure in securing the EMEA CEO role. While her line-manager and the group HR director both knew about the coaching and were happy for it to go ahead, it was essentially a process she commissioned and organized for herself.

Preparing for the first meeting

Following my initial telephone conversation with Nicola, over a month went by before her personal assistant contacted my office to arrange our first session. When we spoke, Nicola had been keen to meet as soon as possible, so I was a little surprised at this unexplained delay. I wondered whether there was a connection between the coaching issue that she had identified and her slowness in arranging the appointment. An individual who found it hard to engage sufficiently with her colleagues might well have mixed feelings about the intimacy of the coaching relationship. I suspected that the delay in arranging our meeting reflected a degree of ambivalence. In particular, I guessed, Nicola might be concerned about whether I would be too intrusive or too touchy-feely for her taste. When we met, it would be important to bear this possibility in mind.

The coaching challenge

During our call, Nicola had impressed me with her clear, concise analysis of the 360-degree feedback and her determination to tackle the issues that it had raised. She had been direct, professional and businesslike. I could imagine that at her best she would provide strong leadership, characterized by a calm, objective, task-focused approach (the profile at the bottom right of the triangle in EPT terms). Under pressure or stress, however, this profile led such leaders to *freeze*. They often shifted from a highly functional if unemotional style to a dysfunctional loss of capacity to relate emotionally to others.

If I was right, my challenge would be to build a working alliance with Nicola that respected her discomfort with emotion and need for distance while getting close enough to help her make some internal and external changes. If I failed to consider sufficiently her wish for privacy and tight control of her personal boundaries, I would almost certainly trigger a defensive reaction. On the other hand, if I did not create sufficient trust and a close enough emotional connection, I would be unlikely to be able to help her become more tolerant of and in touch with her own and other people's feelings.

Containing anxiety

Nicola made a striking first impression. A tall, slim woman with short blonde hair and designer glasses, she conveyed a sense of elegance and poise. She chatted easily as we went upstairs to the coaching room. Once settled, I said it was good to meet her and that I looked forward to hearing more about her thinking in relation to the coaching process. In particular, it would be helpful to hear more about what she would regard as a successful outcome. What were her specific objectives? How would she and others know that she had achieved them?

In opening our conversation, I was aware of using language that was precise and businesslike and terms like 'think' rather than 'feel'. This was both instinctive and the result of my preparation for this meeting. I wanted to match Nicola's own rational, unemotional style to reduce her anxiety about the coaching process. My more natural approach would be to ask open questions at the outset so as to understand more about the client's background, experience, current role and organizational issues. However, given her profile, I decided that starting with a focused approach on what she would like to achieve through coaching would give her a greater sense of control over our discussion and reassure her that we were there to achieve a task and not just chat.

Exploring the coaching issue

Nicola explained that she regarded herself as a successful leader – logical, analytical and good at seeing the big picture. She thought her signature strength was the capacity to envision where the business should be going and then ensuring that the steps needed to implement it were taken as effectively as possible. She liked developing new ideas and initiatives and acknowledged that routine people management was not something she particularly enjoyed.

She was open about her ambition to move into her boss's role, which she saw as an exciting challenge. She considered her main competitor for the job to be weaker than her in the strategic and analytical arenas but knew that he was regarded as having excellent people skills. These would be particularly relevant in the EMEA role, which involved managing a multicultural group of country heads. She felt that her perceived weakness in this area could lead to her being passed over, despite the excellent results that the UK business had achieved since she had become managing director.

When I asked how she felt about the feedback she had achieved, Nicola explained that she had received similar feedback in the past about being too reserved and needing to spend more time developing her team. In response, she had bought and read several books on people management and the psychology of motivation and had made an effort over the past couple of years to invest more time in relationships at work. She held regular team meetings and monthly one-to-one sessions with her direct reports and had put some informal contact time with peers in her diary. She had thought that this had addressed the issue and was therefore quite shocked at the extent to which these themes had re-emerged in her latest 360-degree feedback data. She expressed some frustration too as if she was asking herself, 'what more do people want from me?'

Despite this surprise and frustration, Nicola had accepted that this aspect of her leadership needed more attention. She acknowledged that she had always found it difficult to open up in a relaxed way except with a small circle of close friends and family. She commented rather wistfully that she envied one of the other country managing directors who was able to show an easy, natural interest in others: 'He is always relaxed and friendly and manages to draw anybody out, whether on work-related or social topics. Everyone warms to him. He makes it look so easy.'

As well as the themes contained in the 360-degree data, Nicola had also become more aware of the issue of her emotional engagement through feedback from other participants on the Harvard programme and I asked her to tell me more about this. It emerged that her classmates had given her positive feedback in her areas of strength. However, when the members of her project team gave each other constructive criticism, one had described Nicola as 'a bit of an ice queen'. This teammate explained that she found Nicola pleasant and professional but unwilling to share much about herself, which made her difficult to get to know. At times she appeared almost 'too perfect', as she appeared to have no weaknesses or vulnerabilities and this could create a distance and even make her slightly intimidating. These comments were confirmed by others in the group and echoed the themes in her 360-degree data.

Digging deeper

Listening to Nicola, a number of questions came to mind. I wanted to explore why her conscious efforts to engage more with her colleagues were not working as well as she had hoped, so I asked her to tell me about the one-to-one sessions she had with her direct reports. It emerged that these meetings were task-focused occasions on which they would discuss the work on the individual's current agenda. I asked Nicola how she felt about the idea of coaching her direct reports to help them improve their skills over time and giving them regular feedback on their performance. She replied that she felt that her team members were experienced, senior managers who should know how to do their jobs. She did not think that they would or should need 'patting on the head' or 'telling off'. For her part, she welcomed the fact that her boss left her to get on with her job and insisted that she would feel patronized if he 'breathed down her neck'.

When I enquired about Nicola's social interactions with colleagues, she told me that she made a point of remembering to ask how people's weekends or holidays had gone and to take a few minutes to chat socially at the beginning or end of one-to-one meetings. When I asked how much of her own news she would share, the answer was 'probably not much'. She explained that she had always operated on the principle of keeping work and personal affairs separate and that being professional meant 'not spilling your private life all over the office'. Most people in the office would not be interested anyway, she added, but in her experience there were always some who 'want to know every detail and couldn't be trusted not to gossip'.

I also wanted to understand why Nicola thought that she had received low 360 scores about her ability to create an 'inspiring vision' when she was clearly good at seeing the big picture. This had also puzzled Nicola but when we explored the question, it emerged that this too related to a lack of emotional connection. She confirmed that she had a clear vision of where she thought the UK business should go but admitted that she probably did not communicate it widely enough. I asked her to communicate it to me so that I could gain a feel for *how* it came across. This was revealing, as Nicola focused on targets and goals almost entirely in terms of facts and figures and presented them in a low-key, almost monotone style. While the content of her message made excellent sense, it was delivered without passion and I did not feel emotionally engaged or excited by the picture she outlined of what the business could achieve.

Finally, I asked Nicola how she thought she behaved when under particular pressure or when feeling stressed, as she had received feedback that she both retreated from her team members and became something of a micromanager. She replied that she coped well with pressure. Unlike some of her colleagues, she had the capacity to remain calm and unflustered in a crisis. She described her ability to take an objective view of a difficult issue or situation and to analyse quickly what needed to be done. Her focus would then close in on the tasks that needed to be undertaken by her and by her team members.

Before challenging Nicola about the possible downside of this approach, I wanted to affirm the strengths that it reflected. I commented on the value of her capacity to stay calm and cool when others around her might be anxious or even panicking. I went on to raise the feedback she had received and asked how she thought her colleagues might experience her when she was in this hyper-focused state. Nicola acknowledged that she could understand that she might appear somewhat unavailable or remote during these periods of pressure, but insisted that her team members should surely realize that she was simply doing her job as a leader and taking responsibility for sorting out a problem.

Building a working alliance

Most of our first meeting was taken up with Nicola's explanation of her key issues. I felt that I had usefully dug a little deeper and had gained a clear sense of her profile, strengths and development needs. However, our interaction felt as if it had taken place almost entirely at a cognitive level. While this had worked well as a strategy to provide Nicola with a sense of psychological safety and control – and the information I had gained was both useful and important – I felt the need to redirect my focus if we were to build a strong working alliance.

With a task-focused, achievement-oriented client such as Nicola, I felt it was essential that she experienced me as being tough enough not to take everything she said at face value. She needed to respect my ability to push her beyond her comfort zone – in a sense to pierce her protective coating. Yet, given her anxiety around emotions, intimacy and intrusion, it was vital that she also experienced me as a containing not threatening presence and as someone whom she could trust not to violate her boundaries.

Bearing in mind the need to tread carefully, I decided to try and create a stronger connection with Nicola by verbalizing her *mixed feelings* about the issues we had been discussing, as I had done with Daniel. This technique would enable me to test out how easily I could extend her self-awareness. It would also help her realize that my own thinking and analysis would form an important part of the coaching process. I hoped that this would build trust while demonstrating to Nicola that I could add real value.

The mixed feelings technique

So, deliberately continuing to use cognitive rather than emotional terms, I told Nicola that I perceived her as having two strands of thought about building closer relationships with colleagues. She clearly recognized that there was a good deal of data indicating that she would become an even more effective leader if she could make some changes. However, while she was willing to engage in this area on the one hand, there was also an important part of her that was less keen on the idea of change. I imagined that at one level she was understandably reluctant to tamper with her current level of interpersonal engagement, especially as it had not stopped her from building a successful career. At another level, there was probably a deeper part of her that wanted to keep work relations task-focused and professional so as to protect her privacy and maintain emotional control.

Nicola nodded and agreed and I gained the sense that what I had said had succeeded in getting her inward attention. She was quiet for a moment and then said with determination that she was committed to making some changes but was not looking forward to the process. I welcomed her honesty and explained that if the coaching was to deliver real value and help her to achieve her goals, we would have to explore what specific aspects of her current approach were working well for her and which were not. This would not necessarily be a comfortable process but it would enable us to pinpoint what she would like to change and how she could achieve this in practice.

I added that small shifts could make a significant difference. Given her career success to date, I felt that it was well worthwhile addressing the challenge that her recent feedback had thrown up, as this would release her full potential and enable her to go even further. She responded by saying, 'Well, let's go ahead.'

This intervention was designed to reinforce Nicola's commitment by showing that I acknowledged and respected the part of her that was less than enthusiastic about the coaching process – I did not want to discount or play down the validity of her reservations through excessive reassurance. At the same time, I wanted to continue to contain her anxiety. I did this by referring, in a low-key way, to the control that she would have over the process and to the fact that our aim would simply be to modify and enhance her leadership style rather than to attempt any major change.

Understanding Nicola's inner landscape

Having drawn out Nicola's views, explored some of the themes that emerged and taken steps to contain her anxiety, extend her self-awareness and start building the working alliance during our first session, I reviewed this interesting client. On the one hand, I reflected, Nicola presented herself as confident and highly professional to the outside world. She had good social skills, self-control and poise and communicated fluently with others. She seemed to have taken the potentially anxiety-provoking situation of our first meeting in her stride. On the other hand, she seemed to function almost entirely at an intellectual level. Both her verbal and non-verbal language was calm and precise and showed little emotional content or range. I could see that her colleagues might find it hard to know what she was really thinking or feeling behind her well-groomed professional persona. When I considered her practice of asking staff about their weekends or holidays, for instance, I suspected that these exchanges were polite but superficial and that she would probably not succeed in conveying much genuine interest. While there was no doubt that Nicola worked hard to do the right thing, much of her emotional life seemed to take place outside the workplace – and possibly outside her conscious awareness.

Anxious or just a cold fish?

This created a distance and compromised her capacity to connect with others. This was not solely due to her preference for being private and self-contained; I hypothesised that Nicola experienced *considerable emotional discomfort* at the prospect of engaging more closely with team members. Why did I form this impression? After all, some people are simply emotionally undemonstrative by temperament rather than anxious about getting close to others.

One reason for my hypothesis about Nicola was her view that her team members would not appreciate coaching and feedback from her, just as she would not appreciate someone 'breathing down her neck'. This statement was made despite data indicating that this was not what her team thought, which felt odd given Nicola's objective, fact-based approach. Her comment had a defensive quality to it as if she was trying to justify the transactional way in which she related to her colleagues, while the phrase 'breathing down her neck' revealed her own feelings about people getting too close.

Nicola's language provided another clue to her hidden emotional vulnerability in this area when we discussed the issue of sharing information about herself at work. Her critical reference to people who 'spilled out' their private lives in the office again carried quite an unexpected emotional charge. My sense here again was that this reflected more about Nicola's feelings than about the objective reality of how others behaved.

In my experience, when a client exaggerates their description of something they disapprove of, this reflects their anxiety about the issue. Consciously, they are simply expressing their sincere opinion but unconsciously they are attempting to defend themselves against emotional discomfort. We saw this dynamic with Daniel, whose reaction to my question about raising his profile within the company provoked an excessively critical response in which he rejected the idea of being self-seeking and political. This added to my sense that Nicola's rather extreme language reflected her fear of being exposed to and intruded upon by other people if she opened herself up to them even a little. It seemed to me that she managed this fear by setting fairly rigid boundaries – around her role as a line-manager, between her professional and personal selves, and more generally between herself and other people.

The way in which Nicola's behaviour became exaggerated under pressure, according to the feedback of her colleagues, also struck me as confirming the anxiety that lay below the surface of this cool, calm and collected individual. It seemed to fit with the notion that, when under pressure or facing a crisis at work, Nicola's default position was to *freeze*. She did not freeze in terms of action; in fact, rather the opposite, but in terms of her emotional awareness and availability. Somewhat distant in her colleague relationships at the best of times, when she felt threatened her capacity for empathy and engagement was shut down almost completely. All her energy and efforts went into addressing the problem and her colleagues became extensions of the task that she needed to control. She found it impossible to ask for help or share how pressured she was feeling. This left her feeling alone with her burden and her colleagues feeling both undermined and discounted.

Using the counter-transference

My counter-transference reactions to Nicola also proved useful in deciphering her inner landscape. Much of my experience of her was positive. I admired many of her qualities, including her clarity of thinking and expression, her intelligence, her honesty about the feedback she had received and her determination to address the issues. She also conveyed real leadership authority and presence. On the other hand, while she was perfectly pleasant, I had felt little warmth from Nicola and did not sense that she had much interest in me as an individual. I felt slightly invisible or two-dimensional in the course of our meeting – I had the sense that Nicola was relating to me in my professional role but not to me as an individual within that role.

Although this had of course only been our first meeting, I thought that my first-hand experience of interacting with Nicola in this context was providing valuable data. It helped me to understand how her colleagues might feel and, more significantly, gave me insight into how Nicola consciously related to herself and others, namely primarily at an intellectual or cognitive rather than emotional level.

In terms of the coaching process, our initial consultation had left me with mixed feelings. I was pleased that Nicola seemed committed to improving how she related to her colleagues and clearly realized the importance of this if she was to take her career to the next stage. The prospect of working with a bright, successful female leader also appealed. On the other hand, I wondered whether Nicola would be willing and able to engage in the coaching process emotionally as well as intellectually. She had outlined her development needs but had shown little insight or curiosity as to *why* or *how* she found this area of leadership so difficult.

I reflected that my experience epitomized Nicola's key issue – she engaged with others but only up to a point. On balance, I looked forward to the challenge of working with this client but wondered how I would help her make the inner changes that would enable her to connect more effectively with others.

Nicola's defences: repression, rationalization, projection

Before describing my second session with Nicola, I shall share my view of the specific psychological defences that she was using to retain a sense of safety and control. First, she seemed to me to be using *repression* to push disturbing emotions such as anger and fear out of her conscious awareness, not just in the moment but over time. This had enabled her to develop a persona that was characterized by a highly controlled, calm, logical and unemotional approach. She remained unruffled in the face of crises; in fact, it seemed from material that she provided that the more agitated the people around her were, the more emotionally distant she became. Nicola's professional carapace also reflected her need to avoid showing any vulnerability or asking for help. Clearly, she gained a sense of psychological safety through remaining in control.

In justifying her detached, hands-off management style, Nicola used the defence of *rationalization*. This involved providing explanations for her behaviour that appeared to be logical and fact-based – and may have had some truth in them – but which did not really carry conviction. An example was Nicola's view that most direct reports would not want coaching and feedback and indeed would find it patronizing. The feedback she had received did not support this view and common sense would indicate, in any case, that while it might apply to some people, it would certainly not apply to all.

Nicola also used *intellectualization* as a defence at times. Extremely bright and well educated, she would discuss the issues relating to leadership and people management, including the need to inspire and motivate staff through engaging their emotions, without applying the conclusions to herself, or even seeing the implications. She did this when she told me, during our first session, about several books that she had read on the subject of motivation.

Finally, Nicola used *projection* to deal with feelings and wishes of her own that she found intolerable. I think that, at an unconscious level, she was particularly scared and ashamed of that part of her that was potentially intrusive and overwhelming. Therefore, she unconsciously projected the urge to intrude and overwhelm onto others whose 'nosiness' she then criticized. This was evident in her comments about colleagues who wanted to know everything and could not be trusted not to gossip.

These defences are likely to have developed early in Nicola's life. When we discussed her background it emerged that, as a child, she modelled herself on her self-contained, reserved father, whose temperament she had inherited, while also being close to her volatile, emotionally unpredictable and at times intrusive mother. This seemed to have led to a deep-rooted unconscious anxiety that if she showed too much of her inner self to others, she would be exposed or overwhelmed and lose control of her boundaries.

As an adult, the cool, calm, self-contained interpersonal style that Nicola had evolved served her well in many ways. Happily married to a man who sounded quite similar to her, childless by choice, she had achieved an impressive level of career success. Her ability to stay calm and suppress her own needs allowed her to be proactive and productive during difficult times at work. It gave her the reassurance of remaining in control and a sense of self-worth through what she was able to achieve and the appreciation and admiration of others.

However, Nicola was undoubtedly paying a price for her inability to access her emotions and share more of herself at work. The feedback she had received from her team members and colleagues illustrated that they wanted a different level of engagement and empathy. Top management were almost certainly harbouring doubts about her ability to lead at the highest levels as a result of this issue.

In addition, Nicola's difficulty in showing weakness and asking for help left her vulnerable to sudden burn-out, were the pressures at work to become too great. For all these reasons, both Nicola and her organization stood to gain a great deal if she could learn to moderate her defences and bring more of her emotional self to work.

Key coaching tasks

So what were Nicola's key developmental and behavioural tasks? She needed to find a way to feel safe enough to make her internal and external boundaries less rigid and more permeable. To do this, she would have to learn to tolerate the fear and discomfort that her own feelings evoked and become less anxious about the threat of intrusion by other people's emotions. Only this would enable her to become a leader who could engage, motivate and inspire her people. I would aim to help Nicola to:

- Become more aware of her full range of feelings, both positive and negative.
- Gain confidence in her ability to regulate and control her emotions and behaviour so that she had less need to repress or deny them.
- Mobilize and express her feelings appropriately at work – about people, about issues, about problems – so that others would see her as a three-dimensional human being, not an ice queen.
- Communicate her vision for the business in a way that engages people emotionally as well as intellectually.
- Share more of herself at work in a managed way that feels safe – disclosing her thoughts and feelings more spontaneously and revealing an element of vulnerability.
- Engaging with her direct reports in greater depth through developing more interest in them as individuals and spending more time with them one-to-one, listening, coaching and giving feedback.
- To identify the warning signs of pressure building up and finding ways to remain connected with her colleagues and involve them in addressing problems rather than withdrawing from them and shouldering the burden alone.

Using the Emotional Profiles Triangle to develop insight and motivate Nicola to change

With these aims in mind, I introduced Nicola to the EPT at our second coaching session. When I talked through the three ways in which excellent leadership could be shown, I was interested when Nicola initially placed herself in the profile at the top of the triangle. She explained that she identified with the focus on task and delivery that characterized this type of leader and also saw herself as driven and deeply committed to achieving the best possible results for the business. Having acknowledged this reasoning, I pointed out that leaders with such a profile, when at their most effective, were characterized by a high level of expressed emotion in the form of passion, enthusiasm and energy.

Nicola still seemed unsure until I had explained the second dimension of the model, namely the less effective and skilful form of leadership that characterized each profile when under pressure. When Nicola realized that leaders with the profile at the top of the triangle were prone to aggressive or critical outbursts when stressed, she immediately said, 'Well that's not me'. Revisiting the most and least functional versions of the profile at the bottom right of the triangle, she decided that this did seem to fit her best.

This process of exploring the three profiles helped to raise Nicola's self-awareness in two specific ways. First, our conversation highlighted the extremely positive way in which both the profiles at the top and bottom left of the triangle used emotion in their leadership, in relation to task and people respectively. While I emphasized the strengths of the calm, measured, unemotional approach of the bottom right profile, this did serve to reinforce the valuable role that expressed emotion could play at work. Although this was something that Nicola had already acknowledged implicitly at our first session, I felt that she was still reluctant to acknowledge the importance of emotion and secretly thought that the feedback she had received reflected a certain weakness or immaturity on the part of her team members.

Second, the EPT enabled us to note the way in which an unemotional leader would move into *freeze* under pressure and, critically, explore in some depth the negative consequences that this had for their colleagues and organization. I talked through some examples of bottom right profile leaders using public figures that we both knew to illustrate both their strongest and weakest sides.

These included Barack Obama whose nickname 'No Drama Obama' reflected his calm, cool and collected leadership style. I was able to point out how positively this objective, analytical style worked for the US President – and also how severely it had worked against him on certain occasions. Like Tony Hayward of BP, his response to the oil-well disaster of 2010 was too low-key. Although he took prompt action to deal with the situation, his lack of *expressed emotion* was negatively perceived and attracted heavy criticism from the American public and commentators alike. I emphasized that, in my view, it was not Obama's task-focus, commitment or concern that were wanting, it was his failure to demonstrate feelings that were congruent with the scale of the tragedy that created a problem. The President's popularity ratings only improved when, on the urging of his advisors, he consciously increased the emotional range of his response. As mentioned in Chapter 8, this was something that Tony Hayward signally failed to do – paying for this failure with his job.

A similar example that I shared with Nicola was that of the Queen's public response to the death of Princess Diana in 1997. A bottom right profile by both temperament and training, the Queen *froze* in the face of the highly emotional reaction of so many of the public, refusing to show her feelings and attempting to withdraw herself and her family from view. It was only the persistent intervention of the then Prime Minister Tony Blair, himself a highly emotional bottom left, relationship-oriented leader, that finally persuaded the Queen to make a broadcast, agree to fly the flag at Buckingham Palace at half-mast and so on. The controlled, self-disciplined unemotional style of leadership that has worked so well for the Queen for so many years failed to work at all on this occasion. (The film *The Queen* illustrates this episode extremely well.)

Nicola listened intently to these examples. They appealed to her analytical, data-driven style and I could see her reframing her perception of her own strengths and weaknesses. Eventually she declared that she would like to examine how she could inject a little more passion, energy, warmth, empathy and enthusiasm – the helpful emotions that the top and bottom left profile leaders used – into her own style. I was delighted.

Promoting emotional engagement

In the sessions that followed, Nicola and I began to apply this strategy to the specific areas pinpointed in her feedback. We focused first on how she could leverage her talent for seeing the big picture by communicating her vision for the business in a more emotionally engaging way. This seemed to me a good task to start with. It challenged Nicola to find ways of expressing more emotion and tuning in more to the needs of her audience but it did not involve the kind of interpersonal closeness that she found so uncomfortable. Nicola's forthcoming annual management conference provided a perfect opportunity to work towards. She and I went over her message and I took the role of a member of the audience, feeding back to her my thoughts and feelings as I listened to her delivery. I systematically pushed her to widen her emotional range by linking the points she was making with things that she felt strongly about, for example encouraging her to re-experience the pride she felt in her niece's scholarship award and linking it to her pride in her team. She pushed herself too and made excellent progress.

Much more challenging for Nicola was increasing her emotional engagement in a one-to-one context with members of her team and other colleagues. Although I had never spelled out my view of her underlying dynamics, I had used the EPT and other tools and techniques to help Nicola deepen her self-awareness quite significantly. A crucial part of this had been a reassessment, prompted by my questions, of her parents' relationship. Previously she had seen her mother as intrusive and over-emotional and had sympathized entirely with her father's attempts to withdraw and protect himself from her. She had now begun to see that her father's difficulty in expressing emotion or warmth might have fuelled her mother's demanding, needy behaviour.

This insight was a breakthrough. It enabled Nicola to acknowledge more fully her fear of being overwhelmed or intruded upon by others and to understand how this pattern had been laid down early in life largely as a consequence of her mother's behaviour. She became determined to break free of this longstanding anxiety, which we agreed was no longer useful for her.

Nicola's new view of her parents' interaction also made her much more aware of the possible effect on her team members of her own unemotional style, particularly when she *froze* under pressure. She began to realize that some of the behaviour that she experienced as over-dependent and immature in them may have been in response to her own withdrawal and remoteness.

Despite these insights, I felt that it was essential that for Nicola to change her behaviour as well as her understanding, I needed to support her in taking small, manageable steps towards opening up so that she could retain her sense of psychological safety and learn that she could relax her boundaries without losing control of them altogether. With this in mind, I asked Nicola to choose one of her direct reports to start with as a case study. We explored the individual's profile, using the EPT, talked through their strengths and weaknesses and identified how she would like the relationship to change. We then choreographed in some detail the steps she would take to bring this about. For example, she wanted to be less guarded with this colleague and to share her thoughts and feelings about how things were going in the UK business – although he was her junior, he was highly able and she felt he could provide her with a helpful sounding board within the team. We therefore planned in advance what she would share and what she would not, including the wording, and we role-played the conversation. This went well and we moved on to how she could share more of herself as a person – interests, home life and so on – with her team in a way that would feel appropriate and allow them to know her a little better. Here again, the key was careful preparation, cautious experimentation in the office and gradual internalization of the new behaviour as Nicola experienced positive rather than negative consequences when she applied it back in the office.

Outcome

Towards the end of the coaching programme, Nicola and I used most of one session to review her progress against the objectives she had identified at our first meeting. She was able to provide specific examples of the improvements she had made in all areas. These included her response to a crisis that had blown up when an accounting error led to excellent profit figures having to be downgraded just before an EMEA managers' conference. Instead of retreating to her office and dealing with the problem alone, she decided to explain what had happened to her senior team and invite them to share their ideas on how best this situation should be dealt with. Her colleagues had responded extremely well to this invitation and she had coped with the anxiety that this new behaviour had evoked, stuck with it and reaped the rewards.

One of the most compelling indicators of change from my perspective was my own experience of Nicola. Our relationship had changed slowly but steadily over the course of the work. I stopped feeling two-dimensional in Nicola's eyes and began to feel her warmth and appreciation – a real emotional connection – over the months. I also became increasingly fond of her, as well as admiring of her determination and intelligence.

Not only did the change in our relationship reflect Nicola's progress, but our working alliance itself played an important, even central part in her growing capacity to tolerate intimacy and allow her emotions to be part of a professional relationship. Of course our discussions were important, particularly to a client whose mind was as analytical and sharp as Nicola's, but the *experience* of a professional relationship in which she could share emotions and vulnerabilities and neither be rejected nor overwhelmed was certainly one of the most powerful elements in her learning.

Six months after the coaching ended, Nicola underwent a new 360-degree feedback process. She came to see me for a follow-up session at which we went through the data together. We were both delighted with the scores, which showed improvement in all the areas she had worked on. Although she did not succeed her boss as CEO of EMEA, she was offered promotion to a US-based role at the same level some months later. She and her husband decided to make the move. Perhaps a sign of what the coaching meant to Nicola are the regular updates I receive in her Christmas cards. She seems to be doing extremely well.

11 Endings

This chapter examines an important yet often overlooked dimension of executive coaching through a psychodynamic lens. This is the ending, a stage at which it is particularly helpful to understand the significance of the coach–client relationship. I also share some thoughts on the themes of attachment and dependency. First, however, I shall touch on the issues that coaches face when a client terminates early or when we need to refer our clients to other professionals for different kinds of help.

When coaching ends early

The examples and case studies in this book have mainly illustrated the successful application of coaching methods. However, as we know, coaching does not always succeed. Some clients fail to engage, decide to terminate the contract early, drop out gradually or simply gain little from the process. They may reject coaching altogether – or reject a particular coach. Some organizations withdraw funding or make the client redundant.

In these situations, and I have experienced all of them, coaches face a dual challenge. We must apply the same level of insight, care and skill to handling our relationship with the individual and with the organization as we do when coaching is going well. At the same time, we must manage the thoughts and emotions that will naturally be evoked in us by the failure of coaching to run its expected course. Self-doubt, confusion, guilt, anger, irritation, relief and regret may all make their presence felt. Yet these situations provide useful opportunities for improving our practice. Having the honesty and self-awareness to acknowledge our mistakes and learn from them is important. Similarly, it is important to understand what factors lie outside our control and to keep a failed coaching relationship in perspective.

Helena

An example of a client who chose to end her coaching programme early was Helena, a middle manager in the retail sector who was being coached by a colleague I was supervising. They had met for a chemistry check that seemed to go well and had agreed to work together for an eight-session programme. Helena had recently received 360-degree feedback that highlighted some development needs. In particular, junior colleagues often experienced her as irritable and moody. Her line-manager saw her as a talented but highly driven perfectionist who was lacking in self-awareness.

The coach brought a warm and enthusiastic style to his coaching. Following their second meeting, Helena had agreed to email the coach to put further dates in the diary. The coach did not hear from her, however. After a few days, he emailed her to ask about arranging further meetings but received no reply. The following week, the HR director from Helena's company telephoned the coach. She explained that Helena had contacted her earlier that week to say that she did not wish to continue with the coaching. The reason that she had given was the coach was 'not business-oriented enough'. Apparently, she wanted someone with more experience of her sector who would be able to give her better guidance on the technical aspects of her job. The HR manager had accepted this decision and was going to look for a different coach for Helena. She asked the coach to invoice for the two sessions that had taken place.

The coach was extremely surprised by this news and felt rather thrown. Helena had known his background from the outset and had not expressed this preference before. In any case, he had plenty of commercial experience, having worked in industry before retraining as a coach. Moreover, it had been clear that his role was not to give her business guidance but to help her improve her management style. He was left feeling angry with Helena for not raising her concerns face-to-face, disappointed that the HR manager seemed unwilling to challenge Helena's decision, and concerned that he had failed to engage this client.

In supervision, we explored what had happened. It seemed likely that Helena's decision was linked to some highly critical comments in her 360-degree data, relating to her interpersonal behaviour, which the coach had discussed with her at the last meeting. According to the coach, Helena had consistently explained away the negative feedback and laid the responsibility at other people's doors. When the coach had gently challenged this and tried to focus on Helena's own behaviour, she had become annoyed and defensive. Despite his friendly approach, he had clearly hit a raw nerve.

We hypothesized that the 360-degree data had left Helena feeling attacked by her colleagues; she then became angry with the coach for not accepting her explanations. By telling the HR manager that she no longer wanted to work with him, she may well have been, probably unconsciously, ensuring that he would experience the same feelings. She did not tell him directly how she felt, which left him feeling angry, upset and powerless – just as she felt in the face of the anonymous 360-degree feedback. We felt that Helena's claim that her change of mind related to the coach's background should not be taken at face value.

The coach found this process of reflection helpful. This hypothesis enabled him to distance himself somewhat from what had happened. He began to see Helena's decision more as part of her emotional response during the session rather than as an objective judgement on his lack of business expertise or worth as a coach. We then went on to explore whether he could have handled the discussion with Helena differently. His own conclusion was that he had underestimated the extent of Helena's distress and humiliation at receiving the critical feedback and, as a result, had pushed a little too hard, too fast. His concern had been to help her take responsibility for her own behaviour towards her colleagues as a prerequisite to helping her make some constructive changes. However, a more subtle, empathic and affirming approach at the outset might have enabled him to *get alongside her* more effectively and avoid triggering her defensiveness. This allowed us to explore alternative techniques that he might use in a similar situation.

We also discussed what, if anything, the coach should do to bring this abruptly terminated coaching programme to an appropriate close from his side. As a result, he decided to call the HR manager but to resist defending himself or going into detail about what had happened. He simply said that, on reflection, he thought that Helena's decision might have had more to do with the issues they had discussed than with his background but clearly her decision must be respected. He expressed his regret that the coaching had not worked out on this occasion. To Helena, he sent a carefully worded email that explained that he had heard about her decision not to continue coaching, had enjoyed their two meetings and wished her well for the future. With this calm, professional tone, he modelled a mature approach to boundaries and did not allow Helena's behaviour to define the ending of their working relationship. This was important for his sense of completion and for his self-respect.

This example illustrates how the client's dynamics, and particularly the anxiety and ambivalence about coaching that characterizes the early stages of coaching, can sometimes cause the process to fail. It also highlights again the role that supervision can play when we lose clients under challenging circumstances. By helping the coach to analyse what happened, process his emotions and gain insight into what was driving the client's behaviour, he was able to regain his balance and confidence while also understanding what he might do differently in future.

Referring on

On occasion, clients will come into executive coaching when in fact psychotherapy, counselling or some form of allied treatment would be more appropriate. This may be obvious at the initial meeting or it may emerge over time.[1] Most executive coaching clients are high achievers from the business world who do not find it easy to consider psychiatric or psychological treatment. Many people still feel that a stigma is attached to needing this kind of help and feel fear and shame at the idea. However, through experiencing a trusting relationship with their coach and developing their self-awareness, clients sometimes become willing to accept the idea of therapy or counselling when they had previously dismissed or not even considered it. In this way, executive coaching can sometimes provide clients with a valuable conduit to other kinds of support.

Over the years I have referred clients to psychotherapists, counsellors, child and family therapists, clinical psychologists, couples counsellors and psychiatrists, among others. It helps to have a good network of experienced colleagues in these fields whom you trust. Sometimes you will need to be persistent in asking existing contacts for recommendations until you have the name of someone reliable and trustworthy to give your client. In my experience, coaching and therapy can often work well side by side but in some cases it is best for the individual to be engaged in only one process at a time. Under these circumstances, liaising with the client's organization in a professional way, while protecting the client's confidence is, as always, an important part of the coach's role.

When coaching ends

In most cases, the ending of an executive coaching programme is predetermined by the contract between coach, client and client organization. A certain number of sessions or months' work is agreed and usually this is adhered to. When this is the case, the coach must hold in mind the programme framework and be realistic about what can be achieved within it. At more senior levels, it is not unusual for an extension to the coaching to be agreed towards the end of the process, if all parties believe that it would be helpful. In some cases, usually with senior individuals, the coaching is open-ended. Rather than discussing the pros and cons of these arrangements, I shall focus on two aspects of endings on the assumption that the timing has been agreed.

Before discussing the issues the coach must bear in mind when a coaching programme has run its course, I shall briefly highlight two different dimensions of the ending process.

Completing the coaching process: review, evaluation and accountability

When executive coaching programmes approach their close, a number of practical steps must be taken. These are designed to enable the client, the client's organization and the coach to review and evaluate the coaching work and bring it to a thoughtful close.

The first of these steps is usually one I take when two or three coaching sessions remain. I draw that fact to the client's attention and suggest that we use the next meeting to review their progress. Often clients suggest this themselves. This becomes the first formal stage of the ending process. In preparing for the review, I look back over my notes and think through the themes addressed and the extent to which specific coaching goals and objectives have been achieved. I also consider the underlying developmental changes that I have been encouraging and how successfully these have taken place, and I reflect on my own feelings about the experience of working with this individual. I encourage the client to prepare equally thoroughly and ask them to lead the review process when we meet. I do share those of my own thoughts that I feel are helpful and appropriate but only after they have shared theirs. This reinforces their responsibility for their own learning. Hearing how the client chooses to express their own perceptions and views, before they have heard mine, also provides valuable insight into how far they have come.

An important aspect of the one-to-one review process is preparing for the second three-way meeting with the client's line-manager, which normally takes place when there is at least one individual session still in hand. The line-manager, and in some cases other organizational representatives with a stake in the coaching process, such as HR, will rightly want as full an understanding as possible of their return on investment. What has the coaching delivered, for both the client and the organization?

The client needs to be able to explain clearly what they have achieved against the different coaching objectives, and how they feel they have changed and benefited overall. Qualitative data including the client's own perceptions and feedback from colleagues must be communicated through a rich picture of illustrations and examples. Quantitative data must be included where possible. To this will be added the line-manager's own views about how the client has changed. The carefully facilitated three-way meeting enables the participants to share in some depth what they think has gone well and what development needs may remain. This evaluation process is often an affirming one for all concerned, if the coaching has been successful, as well as being an essential aspect of the coach's and client's accountability to the organization.

The final individual coaching session can then be used to address any residual issues that emerge from the three-way meeting and to look ahead to the client's future development as well. In preparation for this session, I usually ask the client to give some thought to other possible sources of support that they could access to meet some of the needs that coaching has addressed and to help them continue to develop. Typically this involves identifying prospective mentors or sponsors among senior members of the organization, trusted colleagues, or friends, relatives and contacts outside work who understand enough to be a helpful 'thought partner' or source of emotional support.

The final session is also a time to celebrate the work and the relationship, to acknowledge its ending and to clarify any formal or informal follow-up contact. In my view, these steps all play an important part in helping both client and coach manage the ending of the coaching programme in a constructive and appropriate way.

The emotional process: the importance of attachment

There is another level at which endings can be considered, however, and it is here that the psychodynamic approach makes a unique contribution. It enables us to understand and address the emotional and psychological experience that takes place below the surface – whether consciously or unconsciously – for both client and coach as the final session draws near.

In exploring this theme, we must first revisit the nature of the coach–client relationship. I believe that when coaching goes well, and both parties are fully engaged, it is natural and appropriate for some degree of a mutual *attachment* to develop. After all, coaching involves a series of intimate one-to-one encounters in which we aim to create a strong relationship of trust. Within this, we ask clients to make themselves vulnerable by opening up and sharing some of their most private thoughts, feelings and experiences. For the process to work, coaches must also bring their emotional selves to the relationship.

Some coaches are uncomfortable with the idea of attachment, regarding it as an inappropriate blurring of professional boundaries. I suspect some fear the strength of their own feelings, or those of the client, and so feel threatened by the idea of an emotional bond within the coaching relationship. In my view, these fears are misplaced. For coaching to be truly effective, the coach needs to matter to the client – and the client to the coach – within a highly professional relationship.

Why do I believe that attachment is so important? To help my clients confront difficult issues, make meaningful changes and break unhelpful patterns, I know that they need to experience me as fully on their side. As the example of Paul in Chapter 6 illustrated, this does not mean over-identifying with the client's view of reality, which should never simply be accepted at face value, nor does it mean that I shall not challenge them to see things differently or change their behaviour. But it does mean identifying sufficiently with the client to be able to enter their individual and organizational world, to understand it from their perspective and to empathize in some depth with their feelings. In the course of doing this, I find that I inevitably warm to the client and begin to care about them. This takes place even with those clients whose personality I am not drawn to or whose behaviour I dislike, provided that they are genuinely engaged in the coaching process.

From the client's perspective, the same process applies. For coaching to work, the client must trust the coach enough to share important aspects of themselves and to show their vulnerabilities. If all goes well, the coach will enable them to feel understood and contained and help them to resolve difficulties and grow in their professional roles and as human beings. As a result, while clients often experience mixed feelings towards the coach, reflecting the ambivalence that many bring to the process, there will often be a significant element of appreciation and warmth.

The coach–client relationship and the role of dependency

There is an issue that I would like to address that is closely related to this last point about the client's feelings towards the coach. This is the fear of dependency, sometimes expressed by members of the HR community who commission coaching and sometimes by coaches themselves. They are concerned that the client may experience the coach and the coaching process as a crutch without which they cannot function and that the coach may encourage and exploit this state of affairs by continuing the work beyond what is beneficial or necessary. My own view of dependency in coaching is different, influenced largely by my psychodynamic orientation and my understanding of how human beings learn.

What I would call healthy dependency is a necessary part of any successful development process. In coaching, we work to create the conditions within which clients will learn. We help them to analyse and discard familiar but ineffective or self-damaging ways of thinking, feeling and doing and to develop new, more effective ways. Sometimes this involves the client tolerating acute discomfort or taking scary risks. To do this, the client must depend on the coach – on their judgement and guidance and, more importantly, on their ability to provide steady emotional containment and support during the most difficult moments of the developmental journey.

Without this capacity to depend on the coach, the client's ability to trust, learn and change is likely to be limited. For some clients, being helped to tolerate the intimacy and dependency involved in the relationship with the coach constitutes the most meaningful element of the developmental process.

Felicity

A client called Felicity comes to mind in this regard. An exceptionally private and self-sufficient individual, she was highly competent technically but socially isolated both at work and outside. She came to coaching to improve her interpersonal skills but had intensely mixed feelings about allowing a coach into her world or opening herself up enough to accept help. Sessions consisted primarily of Felicity describing her latest work activities, challenges and achievements and I had to work hard just to get a word in here and there. My experience in our early sessions was of being uncomfortably pinned to my chair by a surge of words and of being talked at rather than talked to. I also felt redundant and rather inadequate, as there seemed to be nothing helpful that I could offer Felicity.

However, through listening carefully and learning more about her history, I began to understand that Felicity's behaviour was not an attack on me but a *defence* against the anxiety she felt about letting another person get too close. I also felt that my feelings of inadequacy were part of my counter-transference to Felicity and reflected her own deep-rooted feelings of low self-worth. Through making it almost impossible for me to say anything helpful, she was unconsciously projecting into me a painful and unacknowledged part of herself that I then experienced for her – the defence known as *projective identification*.

These insights led me not to challenge Felicity's behaviour but instead to allow her to continue to control the sessions while doing my best to empathise and add what observations I could about the material she presented. This decision was based on my realization that, for some clients, the value of coaching lay almost entirely in experiencing the relationship with the coach. Felicity was one such client. For her, the process of tolerating my closeness and allowing me to make my brief contributions represented a significant developmental step. Had I been more assertive and fed back my view of her behaviour, I was sure that she would have felt humiliated and attacked and her trust in me would have been undermined.

Over the course of a year Felicity gradually became both more relaxed and more self-aware and, to my surprise, made observable progress in her ability to manage relationships more skilfully at work. In this case, it seemed clear that the source of this progress was only minimally related to the *content* of our conversations. Instead it was our relationship – however limited it felt to me – that had been the agent of change. Through engaging emotionally with her, on her terms, I had enabled her to engage in return. By allowing herself to value the sessions, she was effectively allowing herself a degree of dependence. Limited as this was, for such a closed individual it represented a breakthrough.

As a result, it seems that a psychological and emotional shift occurred below the surface, not explicitly acknowledged by either of us, which enabled

Felicity to experience herself and other people differently. We stayed in touch after the coaching ended and I was delighted to learn that her progress at work had continued, eventually resulting in a long-awaited promotion and pleasurable relationships with her colleagues.

By arguing that the coaching process should include an element of healthy dependency, I am certainly not suggesting that dependency should be the outcome. A central aim of my work is to help clients develop their own *inner coach* to whom they will be able to look for guidance, emotional support and affirmation. This involves the client gradually internalizing (taking in, digesting and making their own) those aspects of the coaching that have been most helpful. We see this happening through the client's growing capacity to apply the insights and techniques they have learned to difficult situations at work, with a diminishing level of support from the coach.

For instance, I had a client who needed help and encouragement to prepare for a tough feedback conversation in the early stages of coaching. Over time, he became able to talk himself through his anxiety and doubts and by the end of the coaching he had thoroughly embedded his ability to prepare and carry through such encounters independently.

One sign of the growth of the client's inner coach is when they tell me how they dealt with a problem at work and mention that they had heard my voice in their head or reminded themselves of something that I had said at a previous session.

Cheryl

For example, a client called Cheryl, with whom I had been working for five months, started a session by recounting a tricky moment in a meeting with one of her peers. When describing how she had successfully resisted being provoked when this colleague made an undermining remark she said, 'I was about to explode but then I remembered your voice telling me to count down from ten and stay calm, cool and collected so I took a deep breath and decided to address the issue outside the meeting'. I smiled to myself as I heard this as I had no recollection of ever having used these particular phrases with Cheryl but I took this as a good sign. She was evidently developing her own internal coaching dialogue in which her old impulses to react aggressively were being helpfully moderated by her new capacity to take a more measured, thoughtful view. The healthy dependency that had enabled her to open herself to learning was evolving into the ability to manage herself independently at a new level of self-awareness and skill.

Conscious and unconscious behaviour around endings

Psychodynamic concepts explain that, as human beings, we seek a sense of psychological safety, defend ourselves against anxiety and are programmed to create attachments with significant figures in our lives. The capacity to engage emotionally and to relate to others in an appropriate way is a key indicator of healthy psychological development. This brings with it an inevitable price: when relationships end, we experience loss and the painful feelings that go with it. How are these ideas relevant to the ending of an executive coaching programme? As I have tried to show, a good coaching relationship is a meaningful one, with attachment and an element of healthy dependency at its heart.

When the end of the process grows near, both coach and client will almost certainly experience mixed feelings. There is likely to be pride and pleasure at what has been achieved and perhaps some relief and a sense of freedom on both sides at the completion of a demanding piece of work. Clients may gain a boost to their self-esteem through no longer needing the help that the coach has provided. They may welcome the additional time in their diaries.

There is also another side to ending – both client and coach may experience more painful feelings as well. I often feel a sense of loss at saying goodbye to clients with whom I have worked well, become close to and will miss. The degree of feeling varies of course, depending on the individual and the depth and length of the relationship. Sometimes I am also left with some anxiety about a client whom I feel is vulnerable or at risk of running into difficulties.

As a coach, it is vital that I am able to recognize these feelings, and then manage them appropriately. By this I mean two things. First, I need to acknowledge and welcome them as an aspect of the work I do. Second, I must find the right balance for each client between expressing my feelings and containing them.

The other crucial aspect of my role as a coach during the ending process is to understand and recognize the client's loss-related feelings and behaviour. These may include denial, sadness, anxiety, guilt and anger, all natural manifestations of the process of mourning a loss. When the client is aware of these feelings and particularly when they are able to share them appropriately, they form a valuable and appropriate part of a good ending.

However, many executive coaching clients – often rational and task-focused individuals – are uncomfortable with this kind of emotion and tend to keep it outside their conscious awareness. They use the defence of *denial* and, as a result, their feelings about ending the coaching manifest themselves in a variety of unconscious, indirect ways. Here are some examples of ending-related behaviour in executive coaching clients that I have observed first-hand:

- Leaving the coach before the coach can leave them by being apparently too busy to attend their final session.
- Postponing the end of the coaching process by repeatedly cancelling the final session.
- Developing a serious new problem at the end of the coaching programme, necessitating further work or leaving the coach feeling anxious and guilty.
- Projecting their anger and sense of abandonment into the coach through spending the final session demonstrating their lack of progress.
- Punishing the coach for leaving them by withholding any positive feedback or appreciation.

Over the years I have learnt that these unhelpful unconscious dynamics are far more likely to take place when I have not done a good enough job of acknowledging the ending and helping the client to prepare for it. The practical steps outlined earlier form one aspect of doing this. The other aspect involves finding sensitive and appropriate ways of helping the difficult emotions around endings to be surfaced and expressed. I end this chapter with an illustration from my practice.

Robert
This example concerns a client of mine called Robert. A senior civil servant, he came into coaching following a leadership programme that had included an in-depth assessment of his leadership profile. This had highlighted some areas of weakness and he was keen to address them. We worked together on these issues, primarily relating to managing and motivating his team and developing a wider range of influencing styles, for a total of 10 months.

Having never had coaching before, Robert had some reservations at the outset and it took some time to win his trust. A self-contained, shy individual, he gradually opened up and engaged fully in the work. He made slow but steady progress to begin with, followed by some breakthrough moments in the second half of the programme. The coaching became important to him. It enabled him, in his early fifties, to find new ways of understanding himself and relating to others and over the months his self-confidence and effectiveness in his role was transformed.

Unusually, in Robert's case, there was to be no second three-way meeting with his line-manager as six months into the coaching process his boss had retired and no replacement had as yet been appointed. Instead, with Robert's agreement, I had spoken on the telephone to his boss before he left to gather his feedback. I was aware that his boss's departure represented a significant loss for Robert, who respected him and valued his support.

When we had two sessions still in hand, I reminded Robert that we were coming towards the end of our work together. Robert seemed surprised and a bit disconcerted. He changed the subject immediately and did not engage with my suggestion that we review our work together at the penultimate session. I noted his reaction and reflected to myself that Robert might well find the ending difficult. Towards the end of the session, I returned to the idea of reviewing our work and asked how he felt about this. This time he agreed and asked me about how we should structure this process. I felt that he was distant, avoiding eye contact and seeming to approach the exercise as a practical task with little wider significance.

Three days before our penultimate session, Robert's personal assistant called to cancel, saying that he was under pressure to complete an important report that week and would like to postpone our meeting until it was finished. This was unusual for Robert, who was well organized and punctilious about keeping his appointments. On the day of our rescheduled session he arrived a little late, which was also unusual. He seemed a little flustered and launched into recounting a story about one of his directors who had just gone on compassionate leave as her mother had died. He described how he had been able to be more emotionally supportive to her than he would have been able to in the past.

My inner response to Robert's story was two-fold. I was struck by the fact that the situation he was describing was about death. I did not think this was an accident but instead represented an unconscious link with the end of the coaching. I also felt moved by the description of his increased capacity to provide emotional support to a colleague he cared about. Although he did not explicitly ascribe this to the coaching, the acknowledgement was implicit and this was a rewarding moment for me. I suggested that he had in effect already touched on a central theme of our work together and we went on to have a good review.

Towards the end, I commented that it had been fulfilling for me to see the growth in his capacity to connect emotionally with others and that this would be one of the memories that I would value most. Although Robert did not engage directly with what I had said, he listened carefully. I felt that he was much more in touch with his feelings than at the previous session. The emotional turbulence that our previous session had triggered – which had shown itself in his remoteness, his cancelling our session and then arriving late – seemed to have evolved into an ability to stay with the mixed feelings evoked by the end of the coaching, rather than deny them.

. At the final session, Robert wanted to spend time on an issue that he had struggled with throughout the coaching, namely a peer with whom he had a difficult relationship and whom he experienced as untrustworthy and manipulative. There was initially an element of dejection in Robert's manner as he told me the latest episode with this colleague and I felt a shared sense of what we had *not* achieved. On the other hand, as he described how he had dealt with the incident, it became clear to both of us that he had shown an authority and determination that he would not have done a year earlier. I told him I was impressed with what I was hearing and described it as a good example of the inner coach that he had generated over the year. He could rely on this to guide and encourage him to remain both more open and more assertive with other people, even when under pressure. He brightened and agreed.

This provided a helpful link to speaking more explicitly about this session being our last, following nearly a year's productive partnership. I said that I would miss our meetings and hoped that he would let me know how things were going from time to time. At this point he thanked me warmly and in his understated way reflected on how much the coaching had meant to him.

Finally, I returned to a topic that we had already discussed, namely how he could use two of his trusted colleagues as confidants and sounding boards. I felt it was important to make a link between the end of the coaching and a future in which he could continue to access helpful resources in the form of other people as well as rely on his inner coach. Our final handshake was an emotional moment for us both. Robert stayed in touch for a year or so via occasional emails and I was happy to gather that things at work were going well.

This vignette does not provide a set formula for dealing with the end of a coaching relationship. So much depends on the individual client – how much emotional significance the ending has for them and how openly they are able to talk about it. Rather, it highlights the importance of the coach holding in mind the likelihood that more will be going on for the client around the ending than may seem apparent. Through being sensitive to the clues that our clients provide and through tuning in to our own feelings, this last phase of the coaching can become an enriching part of the experience for both partners.

Note

1. For common psychological issues that may indicate the need to refer a client on, see Buckley and Buckley, 2006.

Afterword

Writing about my practice after many years in the field has been a challenging yet ultimately enjoyable experience. As I work intuitively with my clients, the process of having to analyse in detail what I do and why I do it has not always been easy. I know that it has helped me to become a better coach, supervisor and teacher. Bringing the book to a close is one of those moments of mixed feelings that I have frequently referred to in the text. It does not feel so different from finishing a long and difficult piece of coaching with a client to whom I am attached and committed, yet whose stop–start progress has from time to time thrown me into painful states of frustration and self-doubt! In the same way that I sometimes think a client would benefit from just one or two more sessions, a part of me feels that if I could just keep writing a little longer, the result would be better. Fortunately, seasoned editors and the boundaries set by the demands of the real world help me to let go.

I close with the hope that this book has proved thought provoking and helpful. I have done my best to bring alive the executive coaching process and to make the case for a psychodynamic approach. If it inspires you to use some of the concepts and methods described to enhance your own practice, or to research this approach further, it will have achieved its purpose.

Bibliography

Armstrong, D. (2005) *Organization in the Mind: Psychoanalysis, Group Relations, and Organizational Consultancy*. London: Karnac Books.

Babiak, P. and Hare, R.D. (2007) *Snakes in Suits: When Psychopaths Go to Work*. London: HarperCollins.

Bion, W.R. (1961) *Experiences in Groups and Other Papers*. London: Tavistock Publications.

Bion, W.R. (1962) A theory of thinking, in *Second Thoughts*. London: Karnac Books.

Bridges, W. (2002) *Managing Transitions: Making the Most of Change*. London: Nicholas Brealey Publishing.

Brunning, H. (ed.) (2006) *Executive Coaching: Systems Psychodynamic Perspective*. London: Karnac Books.

Buckley, A. and Buckley, C. (2006) *A Guide to Coaching and Mental Health: The Recognition and Management of Psychological Issues*. Hove, UK: Routledge.

Casemore, R., Dyos, G., Eden, A., Kellner, K., McAuley, J. and Moss, S. (eds.) (1994) *What Makes Consultancy Work: Understanding the Dynamics*. London: South Bank University Press.

CIPD (Chartered Institute of Personnel and Development) (2009) *Taking the Temperature of Coaching*, Report, 24 September. London: CIPD.

Colman, A.D. and Bexton, W.H. (1975) *Group Relations Reader 1*. Washington, DC: A.K. Rice Institute.

Czander, W.M. (1993) *The Psychodynamics of Work and Organizations: Theory and Application*. New York: Guilford Press.

Damasio, A. (2006) *Descartes' Error*. London: Vintage.

Fonagy, P. (2001) *Attachment Theory and Psychoanalysis*. London: Karnac Books.

Freud, S. (1991) *The Essentials of Psycho-Analysis: The Definitive Collection of Sigmund Freud's Writing*. London: Penguin.

Freud, S. (2006) *The Penguin Freud Reader*. London: Penguin.

Gay, P. (1995) *The Freud Reader*. New York: W.W. Norton.

Gerhardt, S. (2004) *Why Love Matters: How Affection Shapes a Baby's Brain*. Hove, UK: Brunner-Routledge.

Gladwell, M. (2006) *Blink: The Power of Thinking without Thinking*. London: Penguin.

Goleman, D. (1996) *Emotional Intelligence: Why it can Matter More Than IQ*. London: Bloomsbury.

Goleman, D. (2006) *Working with Emotional Intelligence*. New York: Bantam Dell.

Goleman, D., Boyatzis, R. and McKee, A. (2001) Primal leadership: the hidden driver of great performance, *Harvard Business Review*, December, pp. 42–51.

Hawkins, P. and Shohet, R. (2001) *Supervision in the Helping Professions: An Individual, Group and Organisational Approach*. Maidenhead: Open University Press.

Hirschhorn, L. (1993) *The Workplace Within: Psychodynamics of Organizational Life*. Cambridge, MA: MIT Press.

Hirschhorn, L. (1997) *Reworking Authority: Leading and Following in the Postmodern Organization*. Cambridge, MA: MIT Press.

Hirschhorn, L. and Barnett, C.K. (eds.) (1993) *The Psychodynamics of Organizations*. Philadelphia, PA: Temple University Press.

Holmes, J. (1994) *John Bowlby and Attachment Theory*. London: Routledge.

Horvath, A.O. and Greenberg, L.S. (eds.) (1994) *The Working Alliance: Theory, Research and Practice*. London: Wiley.

Howard, S. (2008) *Psychodynamic Counselling in a Nutshell*. London: Sage.

Huffington, C., Armstrong, D., Halton, W., Hoyle, L. and Pooley, J. (eds.) (2004) *Working Below the Surface: The Emotional Life of Contemporary Organisations*. London: Karnac Books.

Kets de Vries, M. (ed.) (2010) *The Coaching Kaleidoscope: Insights from the Inside*. Basingstoke, UK: Palgrave Macmillan.

Kilburg, R.R. (2000) *Executive Coaching: Developing Managerial Wisdom in a World of Chaos*. Washington, DC: American Psychological Association.

LeDoux, J. (1999) *The Emotional Brain*. London: Orion Books Ltd.

Lee, G. (2003) *Leadership Coaching: From Personal Insight to Organisational Performance*. London: CIPD.

Neborsky, R.J. and Ten Have-De Labije, J. (2011) *Roadmap to the Unconscious: Mastering Intensive Short-term Dynamic Psychotherapy*. London: Karnac Books.

Obholzer, A. and Zagier Roberts, V. (eds.) (1994) *The Unconscious at Work: Individual and Organisational Stress in the Human Services*. London: Routledge.

O'Neill, M.B. (2000) *Executive Coaching with Backbone and Heart: A Systems Approach to Engaging Leaders with their Challenges*. San Francisco, CA: Jossey-Bass.

Peace, W.H. (2001) The hard work of being a soft manager, *Harvard Business Review*, December, pp. 5–11.

Peltier, B. (2001) *The Psychology of Executive Coaching: Theory and Application*. New York: Brunner-Routledge.

Rogers, J. (2004) *Coaching Skills: A Handbook*. Maidenhead: Open University Press.

Sandler, C. (2009a) Give me shelter, *Coaching at Work*, May, pp. 34–36.

Sandler, C. (2009b) The psychological role of the leader in turbulent times, *Strategic HR Review*, 8 (3): 30–35.

Sandler, C. (2010) How to manage leaders' anxiety, *People Management*, 8 April, p. 33.

Sandler, C. *The use of psychodynamic theory in coaching supervision* in Bachkirova, T., Jackson, P. & Clutterback, D. (Editors) (2011) *Coaching and Mentoring Supervision: Theory and Practice*. Maidenhead: Open University Press.

Sandler, J. (ed.) (1989) *Dimensions of Psychoanalysis*. London: Karnac Books.

Sandler, J., Dare, C., Holder, A. and Dreher, A.U. (1992) *The Patient and the Analyst*. London: Karnac Books.

Segal, H. (1973) *Introduction to the Work of Melanie Klein*. London: Karnac Books.

Stern, D. (1985) *The Interpersonal World of the Infant*. New York: Basic Books.

Storr, A. (1989) *Freud: A Very Short Introduction*. New York: Oxford University Press.

Strachey, J. *et al.* (eds.) (1953–74) *The Standard Edition of the Complete Works of Sigmund Freud* (24 volumes). London: The Hogarth Press and the Institute of Psychoanalysis.

Winnicott, D.W. (1964) *The Child, the Family, and the Outside World*. London: Pelican Books.

Winnicott, D.W. (1984) *Through Paediatrics to Psychoanalysis: Collected Papers*. London: The Institute of Psychoanalysis and Karnac Books.

Index